CEREMONIES
for
CHANGE

CEREMONIES
for
CHANGE

Creating Rituals to Heal Life's Hurts

Lynda S. Paladin

STILLPOINT PUBLISHING
Books that explore the expanding frontiers
of human consciousness
For a free catalog or ordering information, write
Stillpoint Publishing International
Box 640, Walpole, NH 03608 USA
or call
1-800-847-4014 TOLL-FREE (Continental US, except NH)
1-603-756-9281 (Foreign and NH)

This book is manufactured in the United States of America.
Cover and text design by Karen Savary.

Published by Stillpoint Publishing International, Inc.,
Box 640, Meetinghouse Road, Walpole, NH 03608.

Published simultaneously in Canada by
Fitzhenry & Whiteside Ltd., Toronto

Library of Congress Catalog Card Number: 91-65054

Paladin, Lynda
Ceremonies for Change
ISBN 0-913299-70-7

---

2 4 6 8 7 5 3 1

Dedicated to David

Thanks for showing me
that I can fly!

Contents

Illustrations

Acknowledgements

Many thanks to the members of my extended family, who have nourished my spirit and enriched its sparkle. Their loving support of my inquisitive mind and their participation in my ceremonies and afternoons of inquiry have helped nurture the seed idea of ceremony until it has blossomed into this form.

I am deeply indebted to Dick Prosapio for suggesting a Giveaway as a means to involve my friends in the first ceremony I created; to Craig Stevenson for encouraging me to put my early ceremonies in booklet form; to friends who reviewed the manuscript as it evolved, offering their enthusiasm, support, and suggestions: Elizabeth Cogburn, Mary Carroll Nelson, and Kathy Herbison; to the fine people of Stillpoint International who said "yes" to my manuscript and have labored with me to make this dream a reality, in particular, Carolyn Myss, Consulting Editor, and Meredith Young-Sowers, Publisher. A special thanks to Dorothy Seymour, Senior Editor, whose patience, sharp eye, and skill with the written word guided the twists and turns of the manuscript into its present form.

Permission of the following companies and individuals to use photos or sketches of their toys or other objects is gratefully acknowledged: to Margaret Walden, Albuquerque, New Mexico, for the earring design; to ©Those Characters from Cleveland, Inc., for Care Bear Character Designs, Wish Bear and Professor Cold Heart; to ©Prema Toy Co., Sausalito, California, for Gumby's Pal, Pokey; to Sulamith Wulfing, Amsterdam, for the design, "The Big Friend; to ©Henson Associates of New York for "Firey"; to Freemountain Toys, Inc., South Burlington, Vermont, for the Vegimal caterpillar/butterfly; to Sierra Club Books, San Francisco, and Princeton University Press, Princeton, New Jersey, for "The Navajo Beautyway Prayer"; to Lorimar Telepictures Corporation, Culver City, California, for StrongHold.

The illustrations in this book are by Shari Brooks, from photographs by Robert E. Ripple.

Cover: *The Sacred Serpent's World*, by David Chethlahe Paladin, 20" x 16" sandpainting.
The snake symbolizes closeness to the earth, endurance, and influence on the clouds. Many Indians of the Southwest believe snakes act as messengers to the underworld, carrying prayers to the rain gods to bring the rain that nourishes the Great Mother, the earth.

Foreword

One afternoon when David and Lynda Paladin and I sat in the tall grass on a quiet Kansas prairie, I took the opportunity to consult with David. I knew him to be an ecumenical and planetary shaman, and I wanted his thoughts on a recent "Indian issue." As environmental concerns and emerging Earth consciousness generated awareness of and admiration for the wisdom of native people, some non-Indians were beginning to take up Indian symbols and imitate Native American ways, and their actions were offending many Indians. Now some of them were shouting, "Get off our red road!" I wondered how new generations could honor and follow these ways without trespassing. What is appropriate for non-Indians, I questioned, particularly for white people for whom there seems to be no respectable white road?

"There are no such private roads," David said. "There are no color-coded access routes to spirituality, and no one can put a 'keep-off' sign or a 'members only' sign on any spiritual path. There is no such traditional teaching. It could be that some white people are seen as having greedy motives that would make light of our ceremonies, and that might offend some people. But that which is truly sacred cannot itself be degraded.

"Actually, everyone is on a spiritual path anyway. The rituals are for manifesting that consciousness—that we will walk in a sacred manner. No one can claim exclusive rights to any spiritual ceremony or symbol, but neither can any group claim that it has none or can't find any. There's no need for this to be an issue. Look all around us here. Sacred symbols are everywhere—and they all belong to everyone! Anyone can use them freely and creatively."

This book answers a contemporary longing. It reawakens and revitalizes one of the most natural and necessary of human enterprises: active participation, through ceremony and ritual, in the processes of creation and manifestation. It is about dynamic and innovative ritual—about creative mythmaking. In this innovative book Lynda Paladin offers us an overview of symbols and scenarios for expressing and acknowledging our aspirations and our blessings. She guides us in the preparation and performance of our own stories—our personal and collective stories. She encourages us to create our own symbols and ceremonies to support ourselves and others in the challenges of remembering or forgetting, of accepting or letting go, of giving and forgiving, thus to better cherish and celebrate the adventure of living.

We long to unshroud our fears, to share and release our worries, to celebrate our joys. We often want, and often lack, vehicles more vivid and more viable than words to communicate to ourselves and to the other players in our lives. We long for real and relevant symbols and gestures to play out to others, and to play back to ourselves, the reflections of our inner experience. We long to share our stories—and, in our contemporary setting, such sharing is too scarce.

Ceremony has nearly left our daily lives. Our occasional weddings, funerals, and services are increasingly intermittent and institutional, and our own roles in these have become too passive. Why can we not participate more fully—and more playfully—even in the sharing and savoring of our very own stories? We feel the longing almost instinctively, as though through some faint and fading echo of our ancestral memory.

Those who have lived before us on this continent and on this planet—indeed, all our predecessors, the ancient ones, our ancestors—conceived and celebrated all of life in ceremony. Losses and gains and the challenges of change were always met with ceremony. The planting, the harvest, the sunshine, the rain, birth and death and all the steps and stages in between were just cause for celebration. Traditional cultures used to be rich with symbols and ritualized scenarios that for most of us are now quite forgotten.

But we can create our own ceremonies, Lynda Paladin tells us, and assign our own symbols—and this book provides ideas and examples to coach and encourage us. It even furnishes examples of symbols of symbols: another object can be used to represent a chosen symbol that is unavailable in a time of need. "There is no wrong way to create a personal symbol," we are told. And we find this intriguing thought: "The subconscious does not distinguish between what is real and what is vividly imaged." Here are powerful implications for practicing "mind over matter"! In this book we are given an empowering synthesis of ancient wisdom, time-tempered tradition, contemporary proprieties, and creative freedom.

Through the sharing of her own personal story, Lynda's symbols become real and relevant. Personal ritual for daily living proves practical and purposeful. Creative imagination, free-spirited play, and even spontaneous whimsy become genuinely meaningful. And ceremonies—elaborate or simple—performed for love and friendship, healing, and goodwill are seen as sacred and deeply nourishing. Perhaps it was the death of Lynda's husband that moved her to explore and experience the significance of symbols in the continuing unfolding of her own life. Perhaps it is her husband who remains the impetus, inspiration, and occasional instructor for her ongoing work. He is David Chethlahe Paladin—well-known and beloved half-Navajo artist, guide, and shaman. Over the years, many across the country have joined in his ceremonies and have witnessed his wit and his wisdom.

In this book Lynda Paladin gives of her learning, and it becomes her teaching—her "giveaway." Perhaps it is a gift from the two of them. This book is at once an inspiring true story, a study in symbols and ceremonies, and a ready resource of ideas and examples. We can hope it will help invoke rediscovery of a missing quality in our contemporary culture. In any case, we can make use of it now to enchant and empower our own ongoing stories.

Doug Boyd

Editor's Note: Doug Boyd is the author of *Rolling Thunder* (New York: Dell, 1976) as well as the more recent *Mystics, Magicians, and Medicine People: Tales of a Wanderer* (1989) and *Swami* (1990), both published in New York by Paragon House.

Preface

Nine months had passed since the crumbling of my world with the death of David, my late husband. As I coped with adjustments and the decisions demanded by my new situation, my friends kept me going one day at a time. To express my gratitude to them, I created a ceremony to tell them what I had discovered about my new reality and to scatter David's cremains (cremated remains). This was the beginning of my use of symbols and actions to affirm changes in my thinking.

When it was time for the Giveaway Ceremony, each of us placed, upon a blanket spread out on the ground, an object that symbolized a recent change in our lives or our thinking. Then we each selected another object from the blanket. Each of us explained what the released object meant to us. At the end of the ceremony each of us took home with us the object we had chosen. The stories about the symbols and the action of giving them away affirmed in a ceremonial way each person's changed attitude about life.

Cast into a world without David's presence, I wanted to transform my insecurity about the "cold, cruel world," a story line within my early mental programming. To symbolize suffering, I used a dragon with big teeth and claws, and by giving it away affirmed that it was no longer a part of my reality. Explaining to my friends what the dragon meant to me helped me release the limiting belief as I replaced it with an affirmation of a reality filled with love and kindness.

When some time had passed I noticed there was a marked change in my thinking. I was developing a more positive attitude about life, and I realized that the Giveaway had helped initiate that change.

A year later, I gathered my friends together to participate in another Giveaway to celebrate our personal growth transitions. This time, I symbolized and gave away the concept of *widow*, because to me it meant *victim*. My symbol was a lace handkerchief, the kind a widow in a melodrama would use to dab her tearing eyes as she remembered her late husband. Releasing *widow*, I affirmed my creative abilities and personal strength to find solutions to the challenges of life. This ceremony, too, had a remarkably positive effect upon my attitude toward life.

Each time I performed a ceremony, I wrote about the changes I wanted to make, the symbolic object I used, the actions I took, and the inspiration for the change in my awareness. Recording them in a journal reinforced in my mind the positive changes I was making. Just as photographs record changes in my life, entries in the journal confirmed positive changes in my thinking. They charted my inner growth. The new attitudes I have affirmed with ceremony have improved my subjective experience of reality.

David Chethlahe Paladin, my late husband, was the son of a Navajo Indian mother and a Caucasian missionary father. He was raised in the shamanic and medicine traditions of the Native American. Because as a boy he lived part-time with the Pueblo Indians, David was included among the children of the Pueblo when they were given training. As part of the *kiva* training, David learned to communicate with the "ancestors," those who have died, who share their wisdom by speaking through the living. This experience allowed him to transcend the traditional Navajo taboo against communication with the dead. He received further shamanic training by the Huichol and Tarahumara Indians of Mexico and the Australian Aboriginals.

David was a highly respected speaker and seminar presenter on metaphysics, shamanism, and contemporary theology. He used his theological training for community service as a volunteer police and prison chaplain, and he taught summer classes at the Iliff School of Theology in Denver.

As a professional artist, David drew upon the native symbolism of his ancestors and from the archetypes of all humankind. His association with indigenous people and their beliefs as he traveled the world provided the basis for the visual tapestries of wonder and beauty he painted with sand and acrylic on canvas and board.

David once commented that I was the catalyst who made his life one of contentment and commitment. Generally, I facilitated the expression of his creative responses to life— lecturing, painting, counseling, and community service. I kept him organized by scheduling his appointments, typing his letters, discussing his next activity. He welcomed my ideas and appreciated my practical nature. His constant companion, I traveled with him to lectures and art exhibitions, meeting wonderful people wherever we went. At home I assisted him in his work.

I met David after I graduated with a B.A. in anthropology from the University of California at Santa Barbara, when I was touring the Southwest with my mother. David had a small art gallery in his home in Sedona, Arizona. Was it just coincidence that my studies dovetailed perfectly with my marriage a year later to this half-Navajo Indian artist twenty-one years my senior?

I continued my studies, and education was further augmented through philosophical conversations with the unseen friends who channeled through him. When I lost David as a result of his sudden heart attack, I also lost the support of these loving friends and counselors. My intuitive resources did not include channeling. Part of my grief was adjusting to living without their audible presence. Because I had earlier asked a lot of questions about the afterlife reality, I now believed David was fine and not feeling separated from me.[1]

While he was still with us David spoke eloquently in presentations as an artist and shaman and in officiating at ceremonies as a minister. After his death I collected his writings and transcribed and edited his lectures and private conversations I had with him. Because some passages were meaningful to me, I included my favorite pieces in the ceremonies I created. Appendix A contains many of those same pieces. Although they have a Native American orientation, I don't feel that I've been strongly influenced by that tradition. I used them because I liked the words and the concepts; they met my needs. If I had married a man from another background I would have used what was available for the same purpose.

Although David had tried to help me believe in myself by encouraging me to explore my own interests and develop my potential, I placed my validity and security in my relationship with him. After he was gone, it was time to apply the wisdom and experience I'd had with David by learning to live on my own and love myself.

To minimize the lawyer's fees, I chose to handle much of the estate work myself. Cataloguing, framing, photographing, and marketing David's art work consumed most of my time.

Faced with the major change in life engendered by David's

death, I explored the use of visualization and affirmations to help reduce stress and reorient myself in a positive direction. My goal was to maintain my physical health by controlling my mental attitude.

I studied the nature of the subconscious mind and ways to implant life-affirming concepts within it to support my new experience. Then I began symbolizing affirmations with physical objects. Later I began to act upon those symbols to illustrate a change in my attitude while a supportive friend watched and listened to me. I gradually realized that acting this way symbolically communicated my desire to the subconscious. The change happened more easily than it did when I used only visualization and affirmations, although they have continued to be part of my mental health program. The insights I gained validated the psychological impact of the Giveaway ceremony and explained why it worked.

When we didn't have the answers to puzzling events in our lives, David's advice was "If you don't know, make up a story!" He went on to explain, "We are the weavers of our own reality. The world is a wonderful place if we draw upon our creativity and recognize that we have the ability to heal, to mend the fabric of our reality by creating a story, by continually responding instead of giving up to a sense that we are powerless to do anything about the events in our lives.

"You create your own reality with your attitude, your ability to heal, and to draw from the mists of the universe all that you need," David declared. "Never have a belief in something that is so absolute you can't move beyond it, or recreate it, or look at it from another perspective. If you live by absolute beliefs, you're doomed to discover they don't work. When they don't work, you suffer from stress, fear, and anxiety. Make up a story to help you move through the changing truths in life."

David's creative approach to life has served me well. The

sound of his drum and his words, "Move on, move on, move on," have helped me continue the dance that is my life.

NOTE

1. Lynda Paladin, ed. *Mosaic of Immortality* (Albuquerque: self-published, 1988), is a collection of comments from the unseen friends who through David imparted their wisdom about the afterlife.

The story
you tell yourself
is the life you bring forth.
Choose wisely your story.
As you tell the story,
it begins to happen.

—ELIZABETH COGBURN,
*attributing this idea
to Leslie Silko*

1
Ceremony Today

Ceremony for Psychological Transformation

What is ceremony? Who needs it? Rituals, rites, celebrations, and ceremonies have been with us from the beginning of human history to the present, from the most simple to the most sophisticated of societies. They publicly mark important events in the life of a person or a group by symbolically expressing and enacting the beliefs of the participants, their relationship with their community and the greater environment.

As humans, we feel a need to punctuate our lives with ceremonies to mark endings and beginnings, unions and separations. A personal ceremony, as I use the term, symbolizes a psychological, emotional, and spiritual transformation. This kind of private ceremony is directed toward the necessary inner adjustments we make when our outer reality changes.

Replacing an old belief with a newer, more constructive attitude helps us realign ourselves with life. Ceremony is a microcosm of reality. It allows us to state how we belong with others, what we believe in our minds and our hearts, and what our attitude is about our life circumstance.

Communicating with words, actions, and symbols in front of loving, supportive friends makes a powerful statement about something that's important to us. The combination of these three elements is the strongest, most potent statement we can humanly make to others—and to ourselves!

In selecting the proper word to describe what I do, I prefer to use the word *ceremony* because to me it implies creative involvement by those who participate in it. Although *ritual* is often used interchangeably with *ceremony*, in my mind *ritual* usually means following prescribed, set patterns established by tradition or some authority figure. These patterns typically resist change. Another type of ritual is the way we begin and end each day. These rituals require little conscious attention to carry out because they are so frequently repeated.

In contrast, a personal ceremony gives us a way to channel our energy and focus our mental intent. Acting upon a tangible symbol helps us to be fully present with our thoughts and actions as we express intangible feelings and beliefs. This unique form of communication sets it apart from customary expression and embeds the message in the deeper levels of the mind.

We need to feel connected to life on all levels: physical, emotional, mental, and spiritual. When we experience a break in any of these connections, we naturally seek a new balance point to help us to feel we're in control and in harmony with life.

Our will to live is related directly to the way we derive meaning and connection with life, the story we tell ourselves. We constantly measure our experience against the core beliefs, values, and attitudes that define our personal world view. Energy follows thought. Errol Sowers points out that thought is energy infused with consciousness. Stress begins in the mind. Attitude is everything. The goal of support groups, therapists, counselors, self-help books is to help us create a life-affirming attitude about our lives.

We're physical beings. It is natural for us to express ourselves with physical actions. The mind and the body are one. When we feel helpless about an event that's happened, we suffer. We experience "dis-ease" because we have lost our sense of control, our balance of emotional and physical energy. Some of us may spontaneously act out our feelings in an emotionally stressful time by throwing, breaking, or ripping up things, or slamming doors. Ceremony links physical and mental expression in a more controlled statement that allows us to express and act out new feelings and beliefs. In situations where we can do nothing but change our attitudes, ceremony provides an outlet for our need to physically act in a symbolic way, to do something about it.

Whenever we experience a transition, happy or sad, a ceremony helps us re-center ourselves by making a symbolic statement about that change. By doing so we understand that it is time to let go of the old and move on to the new. We formally state and graphically enact a new belief, clearly impressing it upon the mind, which then directs and affects our subjective experience of life.

Although many of us may create ceremonies for one occasion or another, we may not understand why ceremony helps us adjust to change or why it can be so effective. By pointing out the obvious, I hope to increase your awareness about ceremony, the way it is present in our society, and the way you can create ceremonies to address your personal needs.

You will find many opportunities to use personal ceremony creatively. By sharing the way I have used it, I hope I will inspire you to create ceremonies to honor yourself and your growth through your life changes.

Fragments of Life

Traditional rituals in our society have lost much of their spirit and meaning; they are often repetitious and empty. Nothing new or creative has been added to more fully address the needs of the participants. One of the major challenges facing us, culturally and individually, is the need to create meaningful ceremonies in our social and personal lives. Our minds need to reconnect to our spirits.

Our society's orientation toward failure, competition, and scarcity creates stress. When we focus upon our failures we invalidate, weaken, and fragment ourselves. Low self-worth contributes to many of our social ills, including substance abuse and high crime rates. People without self-esteem retain little sense of meaning, purpose, and direction in life. A fragmented life is no life at all, but living death. Life loses its value when we lose our connection with our spirits and our dreams.

Echoing the general sense of fragmentation within our society is the way our traditional rituals are fragmented. What rituals we have usually address only one aspect of our lives. Activities are too neatly segregated into groups: professional, political, social, and religious. Fragments of our lives are honored here and there. Rituals of achievement in one part of our lives fail to reflect an effect upon others. We lack rituals that integrate body, mind, and spirit to place us in the larger context of our lives. In this era of high mobility, rugged individualism, and independence we are left to our own devices to fulfill our personal longing for meaningful rituals.

Stress and Health

We are more likely to become ill when we are in conflict with ourselves, with others, and with life. Stressful situations suppress our immune systems and jeopardize our health. The sooner we restore our sense of mental harmony, the sooner we reduce our susceptibility to disease. Good mental, emotional, and physical health often begin with the thoughts we have in our minds. Feelings of emotional well-being promote physical vitality. When we keep emotional stress at a manageable level, we enjoy healthier life. After we've adjusted to the stress that accompanies change, creating a ceremony can help us symbolically affirm a new point of balance in life.

Ceremonies from Native Americans

Perhaps the attraction many people feel for ceremonies patterned after Native American ritual is that they include an affirmation of interdependence and interconnection with each other, the environment, other life forms, the seasons, the planet, and the Creator. In such ceremonies each person has time to speak from the heart, to make prayers, to reflect upon personal issues, and to contribute in some meaningful way. All levels of being are honored: body, mind, and spirit. Life meaning and purpose are symbolically affirmed, individually and collectively. A sense of integration, harmony, and unity follow naturally.

Native American ceremonies involving sweat lodges, medicine wheels, and vision quests have limited appeal, however. The investment of time and money necessary for holding such events make it difficult for some to take part or attend. The terminology is unfamiliar, too. Many people find these ceremonies lacking in relevance to modern-day living.

Initially, I was inspired by a Giveaway adopted from the Native Americans, but I was unaware of the existence of the

Giveaway until after David's death when I was searching for a more meaningful way to involve people in the ceremony I created to scatter his cremains. For my purpose, I use the name *Giveaway* because a change in life requires a symbolic release to mark the accompanying psychological and emotional transformation.

I've drawn from my education in anthropology, my life with David, my intuition, and common sense to develop my approach to ceremony. I'm not an Indian, nor am I associated with any particular Indian tribe. Acting with symbols is common in healing rituals and rites of passage the world over.

Taking the basic elements of rituals that address changes in life, I have created an outline that allows us to use our creativity and intuition to honor internal changes we want to make to help us adjust outwardly to our life experience. Unlike rituals that repeat the same words and actions, no two personal ceremonies are the same because our needs change as we grow throughout life. My approach includes elements easy for most of us to accept, actions that are natural for us to make, and symbols we can readily relate to.

Ceremony In Our Society

In our society ceremonies and ritual generally mark the passage of time, special events, or significant changes in status or profession, or else they reflect our beliefs. As an outward and visible sign of a change in life or an affirmation of belief, ceremonies symbolically connect us to our beliefs and our community.

Marriage

In our culture, a traditional wedding ceremony enacts a psychological, emotional, and spiritual transformation. People being wedded release their single status as they affirm their commitment to each other and assume married status. They take their vows, guided by a religious, spiritual, or public official, in the presence of friends and family. The exchange of rings and other symbolic gestures enact this commitment in a formally prescribed manner. Holding the ceremony in a sanctified environment like a church, standing at the altar or in some other designated sacred site, and wearing special attire adds to the solemnity of the rite to further enforce the importance of the event.

In the case of an elaborate traditional ceremony, the investment of time and money can be significant. As the married pair leave the church, there is little doubt in the mind of anyone who has witnessed or participated in the rite that the marriage is a fact. When the wedding certificate is signed, witnessed, and legally recorded, it is official. Festivities at the wedding reception further support the couple's status and link the married pair to their community of friends and family. Other rituals include cutting the wedding cake, giving gifts, toasting the couple, and throwing the bouquet and the garter. Nowadays, people planning weddings often compose new rituals, new ways of symbolizing their commitment, that are particularly meaningful to them personally.

The ceremony changes the way the newly-married pair behave with each other and the way they are treated within their community. The bride may confirm her status by changing her name. Living together and wearing a wedding ring becomes an ever-present symbolic affirmation of the event and of commitment to each other. The ceremony of spoken vows accompanied by actions with symbols has created a psycho-

7

logical, emotional, and spiritual transformation, a change of status, a new way of living within society.

Certificates, Uniforms, and Titles

In this society, certificates formally document completion. The degree of ritual involved, the place the ritual is held, and the way the certificate is presented are important factors in recognizing the change in status. Divorce decrees and death certificates are typically presented unceremoniously. An officially signed and witnessed document symbolizes the completion of a process, whether it is education, divorce, or death. The certificate makes it an accomplished fact.

Report cards, diplomas, and licenses testify that we've passed the test, made the grade, or become proficient in an aspect of training or education. Or they can document events in the life cycle, like birth, adoption, baptism, marriage, and death. On most occasions, these transitions are witnessed by the community of friends, family, and peers. In wedding and graduation ceremonies, those making the change wear special clothing. The words spoken in a formal address engender hope and inspiration and create a sense of expectancy and empowerment for those who are honored. A formal printed announcement and/or business card affirms the changed status. A new professional title reflects formal training and becomes linked with the individual's identity and self-esteem. In some cases, the manner of dress changes, as in the medical profession. Military uniforms denote rank and status. Changing clothes at the end of the work day signals a change of focus and activity.

Ceremonies, certificates, titles, and manner of dress make clear to our minds that a change has been made in our lives. Our participation in a formal ceremony affirms the change and directs our minds to new patterns of thought. Ceremonies mark completions and new beginnings.

Ceremony and Human Need

The prevalence of clubs, service organizations, and public and private societies, as well as religious and fraternal organizations, is a testament to our need to join others with similar interests and beliefs. In many groups ceremony links members to a particular belief and to each other. Many organizations that adhere to a spiritual belief system perform elaborate rituals. In this case, a member's participation in formal ceremony reflects rank and status according to established tradition.

Effective Ritual

An effective ritual is not just entertainment, but it does put on a good show. It is interesting and dramatic; it involves the senses and encourages group participation. The Roman Catholic Mass, for example, includes drama and taste, with the rite of Communion; touch, with experiencing the feel of holy water and handling the rosary; action, with kneeling, rising, and making the sign of the cross; smell, with scenting the incense; sound, with hearing the chants and participating in group prayers; and sight, with viewing the abundance of religious symbols and special clerical robes worn by the priest and assistants. To distinguish the event from mundane activities, its sponsors conduct it within the sacred environment of the church building. This kind of solemn, elaborate ritual reinforces religious belief at all levels: body, mind, and spirit. People leave the Mass with a sense of spiritual renewal and affirmation. The same thing happens for others who participate in their chosen religious or spiritual traditions.

A good dinner party owes part of its success to the way it affects our senses. Often substantial amounts of time, money, and planning are necessary to bring it about. Considerations include the way the food is prepared, the number of courses in the meal, the way it is served, what is drunk with the meal, where it is eaten, the selection of table service and linens, the presence of flowers, the status of the guests, and the attire worn by the diners and the servers. We consider the importance of the occasion and the host's relationship to the other guests. The combination of these elements puts the mind on notice that this is no ordinary meal. A formal dinner puts on a good show and has a story to go with it to testify to its significance.

Need to Belong

One of the most severe forms of punishment in human society is the enforced separation of an individual from the group. Being shunned or cast out is a form of living death, because the individual is refused recognition or status as a member of the community. Incarceration for criminal behavior achieves a similar end. Being viewed as without status or dignity and being removed from family and community is severe punishment.

Ceremony affirms the human need to be accepted by and to belong with others. As much as we need ceremony, we need community, a sense of belonging and purpose defined by our relationship to community. Ceremony is natural for humans because it meets the need to affirm beliefs and connect with others.

Changes in Life

Many changes in life follow the theme of death and rebirth, releasing the past to grow into the future. Major changes like the loss of a loved one, divorce, the end of parenting, and retirement require reorientation to life. Other changes requiring mental adjustments are the loss of a job, a financial reversal, burglary, an accident, illness, surgery, ending a personal relationship, the loss of a friendship, a change in residence, and a change in employment.

The significance of the change and the individual's reaction to it is a subjective matter. Its emotional impact varies with the person and the instance. In some cases the inability to let go of old belief patterns that conflict with present experience can be a source of emotional pain. When a person is willing to make the necessary changes in thinking, private therapy and support groups can help with adjustment. Some people resolve their issues alone, but in any case, determining a new direction, purpose, and meaning in life is seldom simple.

A personal ceremony created by an individual to affirm the psychological changes in attitude and life direction can help to symbolically restore that person's spiritual and physical balance. Marking an ending and a new beginning, it acts to reconnect the individual to life. Affirmed symbolically through ceremony, these statements and actions reprogram the mind at a deep level to create a more harmonious perspective on life.

Divorce, Bereavement, and Retirement

Our society has no commonly accepted ceremony of divorce to symbolically release the marriage and to affirm the individual's sense of self-worth, change in beliefs, and new status in society and community. The pain and disappointment of such

11

a change may linger in the mind when those feelings are not formally recognized and resolved. Rather than honoring such a change, we often sweep it under the rug or otherwise minimize it because our society expects us to get on with our lives.

A funeral commemorates the completion of an individual's physical life. But funerals fail to affirm the survivors or prepare them for the ways the change will affect their lives. Like divorce, bereavement often requires a change in outlook in order to affirm a new purpose, direction, and meaning in life. An effective ceremony to mark that change could establish the new way of relating to life and link the individual to a supportive community. The same need is present for those who retire. The stress of divorce, bereavement, and retirement can cause illness (or death) a short time later.

Ceremony and Personal Growth

In the past we have used ceremony to mark the passage of time, a specific accomplishment, or an important event. What we have neglected is the change in being that must accompany such an event to signal our personal growth. Creating ceremony for ourselves can increase our self-esteem and direct our attitudes into more positive channels.

Taking responsibility for our attitudes, we can begin to shed unproductive beliefs and thought patterns that limit our creative expression and full potential. Suffering doesn't feel good, and ceremony allows us to transform and release our emotional pain when it identifies a change in thinking that promotes life and affirms what is positive in it. To craft our lives to the best of our ability means revising portions of our beliefs to accommodate change and to harmoniously integrate these new beliefs into our personal world view so that they support our sense of ourselves. Ceremony allows us to reconnect to the deeper parts of our being, our path, and our purpose.

Although we may not always control the events, we choose our attitudes about them. Our experience of life is relative and subjective. The attitudes we adopt tend to support our self-image, whether that image is negative or positive. The general story we tell ourselves about life and our relationship with it is based upon our programmed beliefs, our value system, and our perception of past experience.

Some changes in our lives are emotionally charged and highly valued. Usually, these are issues involving self-esteem, relationships, family, health, work, and money. Big changes in life affect all levels of our lives, frequently provoking a reevaluation of beliefs, values, and purpose. A personal ceremony can help us reorder our sense of life.

When something happens to us that has no apparent purpose or meaning (like illness, an accident, or the sudden death of a loved one) it is natural to feel loss, emotional pain, and grief. The event conflicts directly with the way we believe life should be. Bad things shouldn't happen to good people. Life is forcing us to change.

Yet even the most unfortunate of events gives us a chance to learn something positive about life and ourselves. Although something has been lost, something has been gained—if we are willing to look for it. Directing our attention to what affirms life can reduce the pain and disappointment created by dwelling upon what is absent or changed.

Name the Change

Personal ceremony symbolically addresses a change in attitude. Identifying the change in attitude through therapy work, through personal growth techniques, or through one's own inner wisdom is the major focal point of a personal ceremony. When we know what we need to change to transform the problem we can begin to act upon it. Once we've identified the desired change in attitude we can use ceremony to initiate the new attitude and the next phase of our lives.

Story, Symbol, and Action

Action with a physical object relating to the change and a description of what has changed is the main component of a ceremony. The story we tell about the change in attitude or belief about ourselves, or our experience of life, affirms the positive aspects, focuses on the wisdom we've gained, and validates us. Symbolic action with the object further integrates these story lines, the new attitudes, into the greater story that colors and shapes future life experience.

What Ceremony Achieves

Ceremony affirms the new belief with physical action and symbols, effectively imprinting these changes upon the mind with a graphic illustration. The mind communicates to us with symbols in dreams; ceremony communicates symbolically to the mind in its own special language to create changes in attitude at a deep level. When we clearly communicate to the mind (with symbolic, verbal, and physical expression), it can easily grasp and act upon our affirmed belief. The mind accepts as truth what we firmly believe to be true. When others witness our ceremony and hear our story the affirmation is real in their minds, too. It's not just something in the imagination; it's been physically objectified and witnessed.

When affirmations and visualizations alone are used to direct the mind, the intent or goal may not have the necessary clarity to be effective. Ceremony, by contrast, is a symbolic affirmation, clearly stated and objectified through actions.

Once we find ways to foster a sense of inner strength, harmony, and peace within ourselves we can deal effectively with the challenges that face our society, our environment, and our planet. When our spirits are whole and healthy we bring more life to the world. Enlivening the spirit, transforming ourselves to full life, we can use our passion and love to transform the world. Planetary healing begins by healing ourselves.

2
Changing the Mind

Affirmations—Vitamins for the Mind

A time of change usually brings with it a chance to review the beliefs programmed into your mind about yourself, about what is important and what no longer matters. How are you thinking and feeling about this change? What do you believe you can do about it? What outcomes play in your mind? How will this change affect your life? Many fears that enter your awareness may reflect past "failures" and limiting beliefs about your ability to handle the situation.

Why is it that our society places so much emphasis on physical health and neglects the health of the mind? Do we need to be diagnosed with a life-threatening illness before we're motivated sufficiently to change our thinking?

Mental suffering created by negative thinking robs us of our vitality and our ability to creatively address the challenges of the present. When we persist in thinking negatively a portion of our spirit, our essential vitality, is devoured by this "cancer." I suggest that we replace the empty calories of negative thinking with something that nourishes our minds. Positive thinking and affirmations are the "vitamins" that promote a healthy mind and improve our experience of life.

Why is what we fear more vivid to our minds than what we desire? Tell yourself what you want in your life instead of what you don't want to experience! Avoid putting anything in your mind that isn't good for your sense of yourself. It's your mind, your health, and your life!

Changing your thinking changes your perception about life. Affirmations are short, positive statements that help transform your attitudes and expectations about yourself and your life. They help you focus upon the perfection of your nature that lies buried beneath a history of self-limiting beliefs. Using them consistently can help redirect negative thought patterns by giving the mind something positive to grow on.

The affirmation "I accomplish everything easily and effortlessly" helps direct your attitude about daily tasks away from thinking of them as drudgery to one of approaching them with less dread. During the course of the day, your mind notices those things that support the affirmation. As the instances become more numerous, it becomes easier to accept the affirmation as reality. Many books are available on the subject of affirmations. Shakti Gawain, Meredith Lady Young, and Louise Hay, for example, describe affirmations and ways to use them.[1]

Changing the Mind

Symbols and Affirmations

Symbols can represent affirmations. A symbol of affirmation represents desirable qualities within us that we want to reinforce, or those we would like to develop. Here are symbols I've used to reflect my values (see Fig. 1):

• The crystallized pattern within a geode, thinly sliced and polished, represents the networking of information between me and others. This networking has helped me to meet my needs.

• An egg-shaped paperweight symbolizes my unexplored potential, which manifests as I need it. The paperweight is a seed of becoming.

• A Russian firebird (phoenix) painted on a lacquered box lid symbolizes my spirit's ability to renew itself after a time of crisis.

• The toy pony symbolizes the wisdom I gather from difficult situations. It symbolically affirms my ability to use that wisdom and to respond creatively to current challenges instead of making the same mistake twice. With an optimistic attitude I can find a pony (the good news) near every pile of horse manure (the bad news)!

• A butterfly stickpin affirms my ability to transform emotional pain.

• A tin butterfly ornament symbolizes my ability to transform my life, to shed unproductive habit patterns.

• A Dutch greeting card design, "The Big Friend," by Sulamith Wulfing, shows a young girl nestled safely within a reptile's fanged mouth, reminding me that outward appearances may not accurately reflect the underlying reality. It symbolizes the things I fear or try to avoid (the fear

19

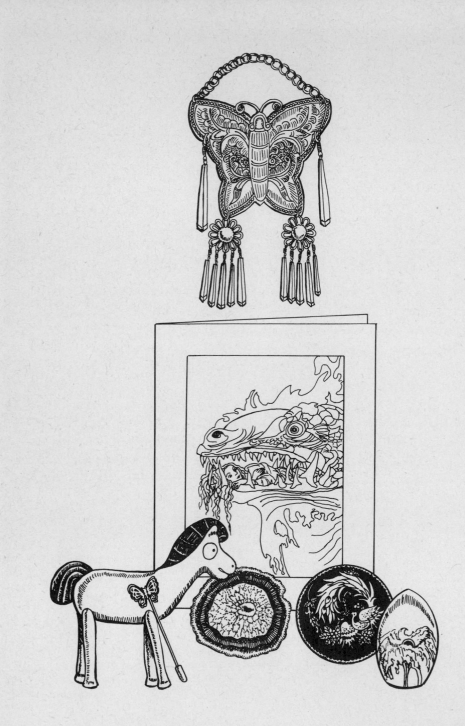

demons) in my life. Usually, facing them is never as bad as I have fantasized.

A friend who enjoys mountain climbing uses a carabiner as a symbol that affirms for him the courage to risk dangerous or new activities and to achieve important goals. (A carabiner is an oblong ring to hold a freely-running rope, one that snaps to the eye of a piton, a spike used in mountain climbing.) He also associates it with cooperation, because the success and safety of an expedition is based upon the efforts of members of the group working together to achieve the goal.

Your beliefs about yourself and abilities are part of "the story you tell yourself." The way you experience life relates directly to your entire belief system, the whole story. Changes in your life give you a chance to integrate new beliefs (story lines) that replace old ones. The craftsmanship of creating a quality story requires continual vigilance and revision of nonproductive beliefs. Affirmative symbols help change these limiting beliefs.

Creating Symbols of Affirmation

A symbol, as I use the word, is any tangible object associated with a special meaning. When it is used to affirm a new belief or to reflect a desired change in thinking, it becomes an af-

1. Symbols of Affirmation
These are symbols I used to affirm personal qualities and life experience. The butterfly represents transformation, while the greeting card tells me that most of my fears are illusory. The pony stands for the wisdom I collect from life, the butterfly stickpin for my ability to transform personal pain, the geode for networking among friends, the firebird for my renewal after a crisis, and the paperweight for a seed of becoming—unexplored potentials.

CEREMONIES FOR CHANGE

firmative symbol. It can also represent a personal quality you want to develop or reinforce.

Any ordinary object assumes a new value when you give it personal significance. To create your personal symbol, select an object that relates intuitively to the sense of the affirmation, focus your attention upon it, and tell your mind what it means to you. Linking the belief you affirm with the object transforms it into a symbol of affirmation. If you can't find what you want, use clay or pipe cleaners to create the symbol, draw it, or photograph it. Postcards and greeting cards may have images relevant to your needs.

Each time you notice the symbol, it reflects back to you the significance you have given it; it's a story container. It becomes an "affirmation at a glance," which registers on the deeper levels of the mind. Handling these objectified affirmations (symbols) with a conscious awareness of their meaning helps, too. Then they become talismans of strength. If you don't like repeating affirmations, viewing symbols is an easy, effortless way to get the message across to your mind!

The advertising industry uses this same principle with symbols and slogans. People buy products because the frequent repetition of the slogan and symbol associated with them has impressed the products on their minds. Now you can create your own advertising campaign to direct your mind to buy "new, improved" attitudes about life!

Keep these personal symbols of affirmation where you'll notice them frequently. At home, a "shrine of strength" may be a place on the dining room table or on a desk. In an office, a cup with a symbol of strength on it can be an unobtrusive but significant talisman. Some cups have meaningful sayings, such as "Success is doing what you love. Success is loving what you do."[2] Change the display or use of symbols to reflect your current needs. This tactic prevents your mind from becoming accustomed to seeing the symbols and consequently ignoring them.

Enhancing the Significance of Symbols

My own collection of symbols increased as silent witnesses to my personal growth. I placed the older symbols on a shelf, trophies of the past waiting to be enlivened with yet another story to re-present themselves to my awareness.

The dining room table is a place that I keep relatively free from the clutter that pervades the rest of my home. Over time, however, placing symbols on the table began to lose its impact because I was accustomed to seeing the symbols there.

So I began to experiment with ways to enhance the visual impact of the symbol by placing it on a variety of bowls and plates. I allowed my inner child to play with them and to select the most appealing symbol container. Placing the symbol on something that increases its visibility seems to increase the symbol's power. It sets the symbol apart from the ordinary environment and makes it appear more special.

If this idea appeals to you, experiment with what you have that might contain and enhance your symbol's appearance. In addition to bowls and plates, try fabric scarves or other woven material.

Could this be why churches use altar cloths? Does this relate to the idea of presenting something on a silver platter? Is this a natural human way to increase a symbol's significance?

If you choose to meditate upon visual symbols as part of your daily routine, consider draping them with a special cloth or keeping them in a special box to conceal them from view until meditation time. The process of unveiling them adds a bit of drama and helps the mind assume a more reverent attitude about the symbols while they are visible.

Personal Symbols of Affirmation

Pins, rings, necklaces, earrings, and belt buckles are personal symbols. We all have favorite symbols, objects, and images that are personally meaningful to us. I wear my phoenix ear-rings when I need to remind myself of my ability to survive the fires of transformation. An attorney I know wears a ring depicting Hercules strangling the Nemean lion—an appro-priate symbol for courtroom battles.

When you're using affirmations to change or direct your attitude in a positive way, you might choose as a symbol of affirmation a piece of jewelry you don't normally wear. Each time you notice its presence on your body, remember the affirmation you've connected with it by repeating it to your-self. This approach is more visually appealing than the old trick of tying string around the finger. The intensity of your focused concentration as you invest the symbol with its new significance should prevent you from forgetting why you're wearing it.

Some Southwestern Indian warriors, contrary to associating butterflies with transformation, associate them with the ability to be elusive during battle. They paint butterflies on their bodies because being elusive is a desirable characteristic. Sym-bols mean different things to different people, depending upon the needs of individuals and the cultural context. The mind makes analogies to connect inner concepts with expe-rienced reality to provide the symbols we need.

I find it interesting to note the names car manufacturers give their different models to evoke a sense of power and durability, such as Cougar, Eagle, Firebird, and Ram. Stuffed animals and T-shirt designs silently attest to concepts that are pleasing to us. We identify with names and images that reflect qualities we admire and want to claim by owning those sym-bols. Some people, for example, associate teddy bears with the quality of being loveable and huggable. Personal symbols make a statement about who we are, what we like to associate ourselves with.

Mementos of Friends and Events

A symbol connects us to something that is not immediately present or tangible—other people, places, events, concepts. The Greek word *symbolon* is a token of identity, a broken ring or coin, verified by comparing one half to the other. You can purchase circular charms cut in two pieces in a zig-zag pattern. The charms affirm the bond of love or friendship between two persons. Earrings that mirror each other can similarly affirm a link with a friend. They may also represent a shared special experience, like a ceremony, with a friend. If each person keeps one of a pair of earrings, both have matching tokens that connect them to each other and to the memory of the ceremony.

Trophy/Treasure

A trophy or a medal is the outward physical shape for a symbol of victory. Sports participants display trophies and medals that document their achievements. The treasure underlies the more obvious outer symbolism. Athletes need many personal strengths (the treasure) to achieve the goal of competition: courage, perseverance, patience, skill, physical strength, stamina, belief in themselves.

We connect our accomplishments with certificates and other symbols of those events. These are the trophies. Give these trophies a new dimension by thinking about the skills you needed to learn, the inner resources you used to achieve the goal, and the insights you gained about yourself during the process. Then your trophy can reflect its inner treasure, a reminder of your personal strengths. Whether or not your trophy hangs on the wall, keep its treasure in your heart to empower your spirit!

Symbols of Release

Some personal symbols need to be transformed. These may relate to a painful emotional experience and the desire to release the pain they symbolize. After a divorce, for example, the wedding ring can be melted down and reshaped to affirm the individual. Whatever the pain, it needs to be honored because it has taught you something about yourself and your attitude about life, your expectations about it.

Symbols of release are followed naturally by symbols of affirmation, which direct the attention to the next phase or new attitude. As the old belief is symbolically released a new belief replaces it. A symbol of release can mark the end of a cycle and affirm the beginning of a new one. In the example above, the old symbol of marriage is released by transforming the ring into something more personally meaningful: a symbol of affirmation.

The Demon and the Daisy: a Healing Ceremony

The following story illustrates the way I created a personal ceremony to change my mind and heal my heart.

Many years ago I had some personally painful experiences with a woman whom I'd believed to be my friend. The old hurt surfaced when I learned she wanted to meet with me at a reception we were both to attend.

Here was a chance for me to put my theory to work to heal the pain from an unpleasant event—a personal "demon." After working through the emotional pain and carefully thinking it through, I was able to forgive her and let go of the bitterness and resentment contained in the old grudge. A feeling of peace grew in my heart where the bad feelings had been before.

Enlightened healers working with patients who have

had spontaneous remissions attribute those remissions in part to the individual's ability to resolve inner conflicts and pain collected from the past. Elisabeth Kubler-Ross (*On Death and Dying*) calls this taking care of unfinished business. Stephen Levine, author of *Healing into Life & Death* and other books about death and dying, encourages the sick and terminally ill who come to him to "soften" the heart, to forgive others for the mental pain of the past.[3] Healing must begin on the heart level. Love and forgiveness soften the heart. When the pain can be accepted, it can be released. Viewing individual pain as a shared, general human pain helps with the release. It then becomes not "*my* pain" but "*the* pain."

The meeting with the woman who had hurt me was still to come. Could I be absolutely certain when I stood face to face with her that I would not slip back into the old way of thinking? What significant action could I perform to symbolize this change of mind and further embed it in my heart?

Thinking it over, listening for a sense of intuitive "rightness" in my mind, I finally decided upon a white rose to symbolize the anger-free state of my heart. By then, however, it was the day of the reception, a Sunday, and I was unfamiliar with the town; chances were slim I could locate what I needed.

I found a grocery store that sold flowers, but it had no white roses. A red rose was an unacceptable substitute because, in this case, for me red symbolized anger. Instead, I chose a sprig of white daisies. I decided the yellow centers symbolized the sunshine of my spirit, surrounded by the white petals of the anger-free purity of my heart. Then I stopped at the cookie bin and selected two chocolate chip cookies. They would symbolize food for the body to accompany the "spirit food" of the daisies. Carol had enjoyed cookies I'd baked and shared with her as symbols of love when we were friends so long ago. Although we'd both been changed by the years, we recognized each other instantly when we met at the reception. I excused myself from the other guests, grabbed my symbols, and walked with Carol to the shade of a tree, where we could talk privately.

I told her how much I admired her courage for initiating the meeting, and then I let her talk. When she had finished unburdening herself, I told her I bore no malice in my heart, affirming it with a hearty embrace.

Then it was my turn to express my thoughts and feelings. I told her how I had envisioned the meeting as an opportunity to face a "demon" from the past. Laughing, I told her she didn't fit the description very well. I explained how my thinking had evolved to allow me to release the pain. To symbolize the purity of my heart I asked her to pretend the rapidly wilting daisies were a white rose I offered to her. Catching on to her role in my ceremony, she gladly and solemnly accepted the "white rose." I ended the ceremony with a cookie communion to symbolize the good times we'd shared in the past and to affirm the renewal of our friendship. After having a photograph taken together to mark the occasion, we embraced once more and went our separate ways.

Checking on an intuitive level within myself, I found no sign of the "demon." The spur-of-the-moment ceremony I had devised to heal the hurt from an old wound worked for me. Whether I hear from Carol again doesn't matter. This was something I needed to do for myself. Any last vestiges of doubt were erased through the use of symbols and significant actions to affirm the change in my thinking. The daisies symbolized my new attitude. Giving them to Carol affirmed symbolically that I had released from my heart the dispiriting feelings of bitterness and resentment, the demon.

When I feel the need to modify the story I tell myself about my life, actions with symbols help make my intention clear. These two elements embed the change of attitude on the deeper levels of the mind because they speak its symbolic language. There is something strangely therapeutic about doing something physically to restore the harmony and to effect the desired change in attitude.

We're Victors, Not Victims!

After experiencing and healing my share of personal pain, I have summarized in this way the elements that are common to many transitions:

> Truths changed
> Wisdom gained
> Demons slain
> Transform the pain
> You remain
> Born again!

Truths changed. We know we're dealing with a potential change in mind when we experience an event that fails to conform to our expectations. Just when we think we've figured out what we can logically expect from our lives and those in them, someone or something comes along to disappoint or surprise us. Expectations are the root of all suffering! Outraged with an unwelcome event, some part of our minds scream, "It's not fair!" or "Why me?" When we refuse to change our expectations we become rigid in our beliefs. Refusing to bend, we're more likely to break.

Wisdom gained. A way to transform the disappointment is to look for what we can learn about the unmet expectations that created the pain. After we've recovered from the initial surprise of unwelcome events we can begin to explore how they conflicted with the expectations we held. How can we revise our expectations to avoid similar disappointments in the future? This kind of revision is the way we gather wisdom about ourselves and what we can reasonably expect from life.

Demons slain/Transform the pain. When we take responsibility for the pain we chose to feel and have learned its lesson by changing our attitudes, we take our power back from whatever "demon" created the suffering. Instead of allowing the demon to devour us with the pain of disappointment, we've slain the demon with the wisdom gained! One of the most desirable survival tools for facing loss and change is a flexible and positive mental attitude.

You remain. Reflecting on life, we find it apparent that we've survived many personal crises. Because we may have barely coped with one event before another (or several!) comes along to knock us down again, it's easy to feel fragmented and dispirited. Emotional suffering can be minimized by finding the wisdom within each ordeal. What counts is not the way we've failed or what we've lost, but what we've gained! Sometimes, we may discover new ways to meet our needs in a more satisfying way, one we may not have considered if we hadn't been disappointed in the first place. Remembering how we've survived a variety of dreaded events, now behind us, suggests to us that we'll survive future ones. We're still alive and mostly intact!

Born again. When we use wisdom to revise our expectations, adjusting our attitudes to be in harmony with the rest of our thinking, we restore our balance and put our fragmented selves back together. What was dismembered is "re-membered" to reflect a new belief. In that sense we're "born again" into a new way of believing. We are constantly dying to old beliefs as new ones replace them. Life is a series of little deaths and rebirths reflected by the changes we make in our minds. Each time we improve the story we tell ourselves about life, we grow stronger in self-esteem and are less threatened by the uncertainties of life. We're creative, resourceful survivors— victors, not victims!

Change and Ceremony

The mind accepts these new beliefs more completely when they are expressed with symbols and actions. A personal ceremony can help restore our balance and reconnect us to life with a new attitude that supports our experience in a positive way. Affirming a change this way can become our personal "affirmative action program"!

The main objective in ceremony is to release symbols of those things that dispirit you and to claim symbols that affirm you. The ceremony need not be complicated or elaborate. Recognizing the wisdom you've gained as you handle and act with the objects, you seriously state your intent to integrate the new story line (belief) into the greater story you tell yourself. It's simple, therapeutic, and amazingly effective!

When an unpleasant event is beyond our control we can feel helpless to act in a meaningful way. We want to do something about it, but there is nothing we can do. Accepting the event doesn't reduce the suffering. A ceremony can help because, although we can't change what's happened, we can create a story that supports our new situation and then perform a meaningful symbolic action to establish a new sense of centeredness that will move us forward in life.

For those of us who actively address our personal growth and who believe that the stories we tell ourselves are the lives we bring forth, creating ceremonies to reshape the stories can be rewarding. We're worth the effort and the time we invest when we feel the need to create a better story about our lives. Attending to our mental health, we enhance our physical health.

Symbolic Expression and Action

We communicate with symbols and actions. Using them, we connect ourselves to life. A hug, a kiss, a letter, a bouquet of flowers, a phone call—each is a complex of feelings expressed symbolically and acted upon physically in a significant way.

We use words to symbolize our thoughts. The action of speaking those words connects the speaker to the listener. A gift usually symbolizes affection. The physical transfer of the symbol from giver to recipient connects the two people. In the absence of one person, the symbol continues to affirm the connection between the two.

We habitually use words, actions, and symbols to express ourselves and connect with others. We are natural symbol collectors and connectors. Our homes are filled with symbols and souvenirs that connect us to other people, events, and places.

Personal Symbolic Actions

Significant physical actions with symbols are graphic illustrations of your intent to affirm, release, or transform what the object symbolizes. What a symbol is made of determines the way you can act upon it. If it's paper, framing it, ripping it up, or burning it may be appropriate. As you act with the symbol, your focused mental intent impresses the change vividly upon your mind. The presence, transformation, or absence of the symbol represents a change in your attitude about life.

A Giveaway is a celebration among friends that involves symbolic expression and action to affirm life changes and personal growth. It is an organized ceremony in which a group of people come together to give away symbols that mark changes in their personal beliefs. The physical action of giving away the symbol affirms the individual's change in attitude.

Ceremony involving others is a powerful way to impress desired changes upon the mind because in supporting each other, we become witnesses to each other's stories. We each take home another's symbol from a Giveaway ceremony, knowing another person has taken ours. The exchange becomes a symbolic affirmation of our interdependence and interconnection. The Giveaway is described in Chapter Four, "The Giveaway Celebration."

Any activity involving cleaning and washing may be symbolic of transformation, purification, renewal. Washing our hair, hands, face, or entire body, and our clothing can be symbolic purification after an unpleasant experience. Putting on clean clothes or buying new clothes can be symbolic renewal. When we change our residence it is natural to dispose of old things and acquire new things to symbolically affirm a new beginning.

For some of us, a physical activity like cleaning house or cooking can be therapeutic because the activity creates an outlet for emotional frustrations. It is a way to symbolically express control over one aspect of our lives when we cannot control what has happened to another aspect. Clearing out the emotional energy permits new insights to come to us about our situation.

Endings and new beginnings involve many symbolic actions. The trick is to pay attention to what you're doing or feel moved to do, because it's human nature to act symbolically.

With the proper attitude, the actions of release used to transform the pain may also be actions to affirm something valued in life. The personal focus and intent accompanying the action impresses and instructs the mind.

Although burning an object usually signifies releasing what it symbolizes, burning can also be used in a positive way. The practice of burning an item as a symbolic prayer offered up to the gods (a burnt offering) is an ancient one. The essence of the object and the accompanying intention transformed by fire into smoke is thought to be received by those in the spirit world. Smoke becomes the symbolic connector between those in flesh with those in spirit.

Transforming a Burden into a Blessing

The personal ceremony described below using symbols of release and affirmation is one I created for my needs. In it I used the energy of fire as an agent of transformation/release and affirmation. My focused mental intent determined what the burning of the objects meant to me.

As I struggled with trying to find ways to sell David's art I became more and more discouraged. My efforts seemed futile. I complained to my friends, referring to the effort involved in exhibiting the art as "the work of art." It wasn't easy to find people who believed David's art was a necessity in their lives and who would spend money on it. A few people who had tried to help me with my challenge of finding collectors had commented that I was not cooperating with them in the way they needed, as evidenced by my poor attitude. Although I wasn't exactly sure how I was sabotaging myself, I felt there was some truth to their comments, because in my mind, the art had become a burden. Listening to my self-talk, I knew it was time to transform that attitude into one affirming David's art as a blessing.

During an outing in the forest with a friend, I created a ceremony to transform my attitude. I had brought with me symbols (see Fig. 2) that related to my involvement with the art. I chose a spot under the shade of a pine tree and asked a friend to sit with me on the ground and to listen as I tried to verbally and symbolically express and release the problem I was feeling.

One of the symbols I used was a black-and-white postcard bearing a design by David called "Mythmaker Stomping Out the Artist's Sense of Reality." The artist lies on the ground under the weight of a strange, towering figure composed of animal and human parts—the mythmaker, standing on the artist's back. This design struck a chord with me in my current mood because I felt as if David's art were trampling my sense of reality as I attended to the numerous tasks it entailed. There were times when I felt overwhelmed by my sense of responsibility to the art. I set fire to the postcard as I spoke and free-associated with my feeling of being burdened. Watching the fire transform the card to ashes, I declared with a solemn vow that the burning of the image symbolized my conscious release of the attitude in my mind that the art was a burden: "I release the pain."

Then, as I affirmed the many blessings I'd experienced by having David's art in my life, I set fire to a card with David's color design, "Sun Gods from Two Worlds," depicting spirit figures of the southwestern United States and ancient Egypt. The colorful spirit figures on the card symbolized the way the art had splashed color onto my spirit, causing me to meet wonderful people who enriched my life in special ways. I remembered my past success with art sales, success that had

2: Burden/Blessing
The card at the left, "Mythmaker Stomping Out the Artist's Sense of Reality," represents my feeling of being burdened by David's art. The card on the right, "Sun Gods from Two Worlds," affirms the blessing of new friends I have made because of their interest in David's art. The paper heart stands for the presence of love in my life, and the dried marigold flower heads contain seeds for new growth that represent my latent abilities.

helped me maintain my lifestyle. In this instance, burning the image was a symbolic affirmation of my blessings and an expression of gratitude to the greater forces operating in my life.

Burning a red paper heart, I affirmed that David's love was

not gone from my life but only transformed to manifest in my present experience of friendship and miracles that added joy and delight to my life. David was reaching out and loving me through the eyes and heart of my friend and witness. I affirmed, "We are all one. Love continually transforms and expresses itself in my life in wondrous ways."

Unscrewing a jar containing flower seeds and dried marigold flower heads I'd stored for a couple of years, I placed the seeds in the ground. I told my friend, "Seeds kept in a jar will never explore their life potential! By planting them, I affirm the creative potential I have bottled up within myself, a potential largely ignored because of my activities related to David's creative expressions. Now it is time to see what will grow from my own spirit!"

Scattering other flower seeds mixed with potting soil to the six directions, I symbolically affirmed the renewal of my spirit and the restoration of my balance. "I sow beauty. I walk in beauty. Let my life be lived in beauty. Beauty surrounds me!"

I passed the remainder of the seeds and soil to my friend so that she could make her prayers and affirmations about her life. We ended the ceremony with an embrace. A drink of spring water was our communion. Delighting in the forest environment, I couldn't resist affirming the obvious, "Beauty certainly surrounds us!"

NOTES

1. Shakti Gawain, *Creative Visualization* (New York: Bantam New Age Books, 1982), describes affirmations and how to use them in the chapter entitled "Affirmation." Louise Hay, *You Can Heal Your Life* (Santa Monica, California: Hay House, 1987), discusses affirmations in Chapter Eight. Meredith Lady Young in *Language of the*

Soul (Walpole, N.H.: Stillpoint, 1987), employs affirmations throughout the book.

2. These quotations are from Hallmark Mug Mates ©1985 Hallmark Cards, Inc., Kansas City, Missouri.

3. Stephen Levine in his books published in New York by Doubleday, like *Healing into Life & Death (1987)*, *Meetings At the Edge* (1984), and *Who Dies* (1989), describes the way he helps those dying and their survivors cope with illness and dying. *Elisabeth Kubler-Ross* discusses her approach to helping these people in, among other books, *On Death and Dying* (New York: Macmillan, 1973).

3

Creating Your Personal Ceremony

Inner Guidance

Listen to your inner guidance as you focus upon a change that has happened (or one that you would like to make happen) in your thinking and, as a result, in your life. This is an evolving process, one in which you allow your intuition to guide you step by step. There is no right or wrong way to do it. What's important is that it feels right intuitively and ethically. As you consider the symbols and actions that will reflect beliefs that will in turn create a sense of order in your life, those choices should also be for the highest good of all concerned. The goal is to place yourself in harmony with the greater wisdom operating in and through you and the events in your life.

Symbols of Change

Begin by thinking about the change in your attitude and your life. How does it feel? Listen and sense intuitively as you think about what needs to change or what has changed. What metaphors come to mind when you think, "It's like . . . ," or "It feels like . . . ."? How would you describe it to a friend? What does it look like? Pay attention to your emotions. How will you feel when this new attitude becomes part of your thinking? Vividly imagine this change within yourself on all levels: physical, emotional, and spiritual.

Trust your intuitive self to find what you need in order to address this change symbolically. Sometimes there is an object in your home that can relate to it in a symbolic way. You may feel guided to find, purchase, or make a symbol of affirmation, one of release, or both. Visit a toy store, or examine displays of costume jewelry to see if anything you see resonates with your need. Perhaps there is something given to you by another person that is connected to the change. Make a symbol with a number of meaningful objects. Give a possession a new meaning. Find something in nature.

Edible Symbols

Perhaps an edible symbol would be appropriate. Bread or cookie dough can be shaped with the hands or formed into symbols with cookie cutters. Or you may want to prepare flavored gelatin, using about a third of the required water to give it a firmer consistency for easier handling. Use cookie cutters, a knife, or a mold to create your symbol. Ingesting the symbol can symbolically affirm your ability to transform or internalize its significance. Taste and texture can be a part of the symbolism, too.

After I lost David I knew I needed to change my thinking

about a cold, cruel world filled with scarcity and suffering. This ingrained childhood belief came to the forefront of my consciousness after his death as I began to fantasize about my future experience. It became obvious to me that if I did not want to manifest that belief into reality I needed to replace it with a more positive, life-affirming attitude. I used a dragon to symbolize suffering.

After a year and a half of identifying myself as "the widow Paladin" I examined on a deeper level what *widow* signified to me. Tracing its connotation back to my earliest awareness of the term, I realized it related to a melodrama widow, at the mercy of a heartless mortgage collector, helpless to aid herself and in need of a hero to rescue her from her hopeless situation. Each time I called myself "widow" I was subconsciously affirming myself as a victim, powerless to affect my own life. When I realized what I was doing I knew I had to drop that word as an identifier.

No ideas came to me immediately about the way I would symbolize the concept, so I put it in the back of my mind and kept my eyes open for a likely symbol. A few days later, I saw a friend pulling a handkerchief from her purse, and my mind clicked, connecting the widow prop from the melodrama to my need for a symbol of *widow*.

These are examples of an identified change of an attitude I held about myself and my reality. I used the Giveaway ceremony as the significant physical action to release both these emotionally charged thought patterns for maximum impact upon my consciousness.

Making a Symbol

If you choose to make a symbol, remember that the process of creation, not the finished product, is important. The creative process is moving from something sensed to something seen. Rather than being pleasing to the eye, this symbol should be pleasing to the spirit.

In some cases you may have only a vague sense of what you need. Take it a step at a time and listen for intuitive guidance. Establish a dialogue between your deep self and the object as it evolves. This process bypasses the usual reliance upon words and logic as you translate the feeling sense into a tangible object. It is an act of faith to openly allow these unnamed feelings and intuitive urges to ma nifest into whatever form they need to take without allowing your conscious mind to censor what's happening. Trust the process and your inner wisdom to guide you. If you feel blocked, call upon your inner child and approach it with a playful attitude. Write about your feelings describing the change, or draw the images on a piece of paper. Then the paper becomes the tangible symbol. There is no wrong way to create a personal symbol.

The symbol created by intuitive guidance is a statement by your spirit, physically expressed, that will help to restore the sense of harmony in the deep levels of the mind. The goal is to use the symbol and the insights gained in the process of creating it to provide additional guidance for the ceremony you're planning.

Substitute Symbol

There were times when I couldn't find the symbol I needed, so I used a substitute symbol to refer to the desired symbol (a daisy represented a rose; a pointed spiral shell became a chambered nautilus). Your subjective interpretation is what matters to your mind; it will accept whatever meaning you give an object. Don't let the absence of a symbol you've pictured in your mind prevent you from creating a ceremony.

Examples of Symbols

Below is a list of possible symbols and their suggested meanings.[1] For the purposes of personal ceremony, what the symbol means to you is more important than its given or traditional significance. Symbols can be interpreted in many ways. Fire is an agent of destruction and transformation; it can mean purification; it can also symbolize passion and desire, as in "burning desire."

SYMBOL	SIGNIFICANCE
diploma, certificate	accomplishment
bell	sound of creative power; outer shell: female, clapper: male
bird, feather, candle flame	spirit
bridge	links separate things; transition between one state and another; change
butterfly	transformation
child	youthful energy; the future
circle	completion of a cycle; perfection; unity
cross	intersection of spirit and matter; joins opposites
cup	nourishment, abundance

SYMBOL	SIGNIFICANCE
egg	seed of generation, fertility; the mystery or potential of life, resurrection, rebirth, life that emerges from encasement; hope, wholeness
fire	transformative energy; purification; destruction
flower	blossoming, unfolding, beauty, love, life
heart, rose, flowers, food	love
honey	first sweetener of life, source of pleasure and energy
key	access to something locked away
moon	resurrection, death and rebirth, regeneration; cyclical nature of life; feminine principle; silver
nest	place of incubation for new life: individual potential and creativity
net	entanglement, difficulty, snare; interconnection with others
phoenix	death and rebirth; regeneration
rattlesnake, tiger, shark	danger, fear
river	flow of life
seed	potential of growth; hope; an idea (planting a seed implies nurturing growth, permitting an idea to take form)

smoke	purification; prayer made visible (tobacco, incense); ash: body, smoke: spirit
snake	renewal because of its ability to shed its skin; energy
spiral, living plant	growth
string	used to bind, connect, fasten, make secure
sun	source of life and energy; constancy, will; male principle; gold
tree	inexhaustible life, immortality; vertical growth
water	source of life; fertility; cleansing, purification

Symbolic Action with Symbols

What needs to be done physically with the object to affirm the change? What symbolic action can you perform with it? How will you release it, transform it, or affirm it? Where will you keep it? Again, use your inner guidance to supply the answers. If it feels right, then that's how you need to act with the symbol. Sometimes these actions come in stages, in which one action follows another after an interval of time.

Symbolic Action in Stages

A woman cut the cord of a string of beads to symbolize the end of her relationship with another, intuitively knowing that was the appropriate action. Placing the beads in a glass jar where she would frequently notice them, she waited for an idea of the next action to take. As her thoughts evolved about the situation she felt she would know what to do when the time was right to act on the beads again.

Planting a seed or a bulb as a symbol of new growth has a number of stages: planting it symbolically initiates growth; periodically watering it as the plant grows symbolizes nurturing the growth; the plant's flowering as the bud forms and blossoms can represent what you're desiring to experience in your life. Your intent and the meaning you give the process is what your mind accepts to be true. It is an "out-picturing of an inner process."

Symbolic Release

Actions with a symbol to release what it represents may involve burning, burying, reducing it to small pieces by breaking it or tearing it, cutting a cord, untying a knot, stamping upon or knocking something down, flushing it down the toilet, giving it to another person or a charitable organization, stripping away by removing an item of clothing or jewelry, or leaving something outside to be transformed by the elements.

Symbolic Passage

You may want to affirm a fresh start in life, leaving your old life behind, by moving yourself or a symbol from one place to another. Other suggestions are: stepping over a boundary marker, moving under an archway of clasped hands, immersing yourself in water (symbolic death and renewal), cleansing, purifying the object, and giving it new significance.

Symbolic Affirmation

Action with a symbol to affirm the desired change or new direction may include placing something on the body (jewelry, clothing), placing the symbol in a special location (altar, shrine), placing the symbol in special container (bag, cloth, basket), an unveiling to reveal a symbol. Changing your name or your hairstyle can be symbolic actions.

Significance of Adornment and Personal Symbols

The symbolism of what you choose to wear is another important element within ceremony. How will you dress for the ceremony? Talking about your clothing's significance leaves an impression on the mind. Even if you act alone, it helps to mentally note what you wear that affirms yourself. Clothing and jewelry connect you to other events. Where did an item come from? What does it mean to you? How does it reflect your personal power? You may want to include special stones, crystals, or other objects that are meaningful to you.

Personal Storytelling

Wisdom Stories

A wisdom story makes changes or adds a new awareness to the greater story you tell yourself to improve the quality of the life you bring forth. By continually changing and refining the story, you craft your life. This directs your attitude toward the desired experience.

Events like the loss of a loved one, a major physical illness or surgery, a shift in professional or personal status, a move to a new location, or a change in life style or relationships embody many transformations within them. It is unreasonable, therefore, to expect a single ceremony to contribute to major changes in attitude. Wisdom and hindsight may not come until you have had some time to reflect upon the cumulative changes. Decisions made under the stress of the change may need to be reworked after time permits greater clarity about the issue. Transformation is an evolving process that involves carefully monitoring personal attitudes about the change and making the appropriate adjustments as the need arises. With a recent change, begin with a short story and know it will change with time. Your emotions and intuition are your best sources of guidance.

If you're unhappy with some event or aspect of your life, there is something you can learn from that event or aspect. Does the story you tell yourself create pain or happiness? The choice is yours. You have the personal power and ability to transform your suffering into peace. You are victor, not victim! You can act to restore your inner balance by creating a personal ceremony to affirm your strength and the beliefs that direct your life.

To initiate the action, ask yourself: What has happened? What truths or beliefs have changed? What have you learned? Have you discovered something about yourself and your beliefs? What have you gained that affirms your ability to cope positively with life? What's the good news with the bad news? There is no failure, only more wisdom to gather and character to build! The theory of a wisdom story is to build upon your strength, wisdom, success, and ability to survive instead of focusing upon failure, suffering, or whatever is absent.

In the book, *Your Mythic Journey*, Sam Keen acknowledges his friend David Steere for pointing out to him that "the common root of 'authority' and 'authorship' tells us a great deal about power. Whoever authors your story authorizes your actions." It is time to reclaim our right to author our personal stories of becoming, stories that shape our life experience, and to authorize our own ceremonies that initiate and mark changes in our lives. Honoring our personal growth, as well as the wisdom we've gathered and the character we've built, gives us the self-esteem to cope with future life challenges.

"We gain personal authority and power," says Sam Keen, "in the measure that we question the myth that is upheld by 'the authorities.' " Keen points out that "To remain vibrant throughout a lifetime we must always be inventing ourselves, weaving new themes into our life-narratives, remembering our past, revisioning our future, reauthorizing the myth by which we live."[2]

Miracle Stories

Joseph Campbell refers to what I call miracles when he quotes from Arthur Schopenhauer's essay, "On an Apparent Intention in the Fate of the Individual." Schopenhauer points out that when you look back over your lifetime, "events that when they occurred had seemed accidental and of little moment turn out to have been indispensable factors in the composition of a consistent plot."[3]

Think about the people and the events in your life that appeared at just the right moment to help you in unexpected ways. Were their appearances just coincidences? By honoring these coincidences and elevating them to the status of "miracles" you can generate more faith in your life. Your needs will be met, and the solutions will come.

As you cultivate this awareness and collect the miracle stories from the past, you can more easily project that miracles will come in the future, too, as you need them. Think of other times in your life when things have worked out in surprising ways. How have your needs been met unexpectedly and perfectly?

Can you identify any strange coincidences that relate to the change your ceremony addresses? Miracle stories of any kind affirm the wonder, mystery, and magic of life. Telling your story to friends who support you makes these miracles more significant to your mind and helps your friends believe that their needs will also be met in unexpected ways.

Part of my personal craftsmanship of life is to pay attention to the way I've found near-miraculous solutions to problems and the way I've helped others with theirs.

Personal Ordeals and Transitions as Hero Stories

Some stories about change can be patterned after the hero story. Joseph Campbell in his book, *The Hero With a Thousand Faces*,[4] identifies common themes within hero stories that I have paraphrased. They are: the call to adventure; the adventure in a new world; allies, helpers, and wisdom figures; tests; magic and miracles; the enemy; finding a treasure; bringing the gift back to the world.

We can apply some of these themes to our lives to create our personal hero stories. This format works best when some time has elapsed since the change so that you can reflect upon the events to see how things fell into place. Sometimes a tragedy or unwelcome change can be "the best thing that's happened" because it's forced us to grow in another direction to discover hidden abilities and potentials within ourselves.

Here is an example of the way I've applied hero story themes to outline a personal hero story about a change in my life. I suggest questions to help you explore how these themes may relate to your life after the example.

The *call to adventure* was David's sudden death. How would I cope with my changed life?

So I began my *adventure in a new world*. Although everything looked the same, nothing felt the same. I met new friends as I called them to cancel meetings David had scheduled. They became my *allies, helpers, and wisdom figures* as I began to face the *tests* my new situation demanded, such as dealing with the estate. Through the *magic* of networking, I met people who helped me with needs as they arose. A woman whom I'd met shortly before David died lived with me after his death and stayed in my home when I had to leave on business. It felt like a *miracle* that she appeared in my life just at the right time.

The biggest *enemy* I faced was the limitation of my belief that I could accomplish the tasks my new situation demanded. As time passed my self-esteem grew. I learned that I was capable of doing many things I wouldn't have done if my life hadn't changed. I wasn't so helpless after all! I also learned about grief. However, I gained genuine compassion for other people experiencing loss and transition in their lives. These insights constitute *the treasure*. My quest to find a way to create meaningful ceremonies would not have begun without David's death. This is *the gift* I offer to others who feel a similar need.

Here are questions to help you explore the way hero story themes may have operated in your life:

The call to adventure. How did the change begin? What caused it? Did you act by choice, or did circumstances beyond your control initiate the change?

Adventure in the new world. If the change you notice is sudden or drastic, it can cause reality to seem unreal because the usual connections with life are broken or weakened. Life may feel foreign, strange, new. You may feel psychologically dismembered. Nothing is the same. How do you meet your needs now, how do you behave, who are your friends? What are your inner and outer resources? How do you orient yourself to this new way of being?

Tests. What goal did you need to achieve to accommodate the new situation? What internal and external changes had to be made? How large was the problem? Was it something you could manage alone, or did you need help from others to deal with it?

Enemies. If the solution to the goal wasn't immediately apparent, what obstacles prevented you from achieving it? Did you know what needed to be done? Did you feel confident you had the inner resources and courage to act upon the problem independently, or did some self-limiting beliefs have to be overcome? Did you lack the required skills and knowledge? What was beyond your control? If the problem was unsolvable, how did you learn to accept it, to make friends with it?

Allies, helpers, wisdom figures. Did you consult professionals for advice about your situation? Did you talk with friends who had similar problems? What did they do that proved helpful to you? Whom did they know who had more information? In modern parlance, getting information from your friends and help from your friends' contacts is called networking—an essential element of creative problem-solving. Did you turn to books for guidance? Did you find in an unexpected source the wisdom that you could apply to your problem?

Magic and miracles. In the solution of your problems did you experience meaningful coincidences in which other people and their resources were able to help you meet your needs? Were some needs met perfectly and unexpectedly?

Discovering the treasure. The treasure within the problem is what you've learned about yourself, the wisdom you've gathered that will help you meet your next test with greater confidence. In solving your problem, what did you discover about yourself and your abilities that you didn't know before? How did the challenge cause you to do new things you wouldn't otherwise have considered? What new tools do you have to help you cope with life?

Bringing the gift back to the world. How can you use what you've learned to help others in similar situations? By telling your hero story to another adventurer facing a similar challenge you may become a wisdom figure for him or her. And pay attention to the times when you've intuitively acted to be in the right place at the right time to meet another's needs. When you do that, you get to be the miracle for someone else!

Trophy. This is an additional suggestion to the above themes that relates to the earlier discussion about trophies and treasures. What symbol can you associate with this adventure in order to affirm your personal strength and ability to find solutions to problems within your life? You're smarter and wiser now. Acknowledge your success with a tangible symbol.

Be-ing Stories Another format for creating your story about a change that's happened is to examine the way the words *belonging*, *beloving*, *believing*, and *becoming* relate to your experience:

Belonging. Whom are you connected with? Who are present for you in the form of friends and community?

Beloving. Who is most significant to you? Are you learning to be loving toward yourself? Where or with whom is it safe to physically and emotionally invest your energies?

Believing. Has it become necessary to make changes in your cherished beliefs and personal values? What beliefs have changed about yourself, your life, and others? Have your spiritual beliefs changed?

Becoming. How does the change affect your personal growth? What new insights contribute to your blossoming? What new tools have you developed to help you cope with change?

Witnesses and Ceremony

The presence of others who witness your words and actions communicates to your mind the serious nature of your intention. It is important to verbalize what happened because putting the change into words impresses the mind. As you tell your story to another, you may make connections that weren't apparent until the words leave your mouth! Telling your story is different from thinking about it or discussing it in normal conversation. Your witness does not need to know what you are doing, or even know your underlying motivation. He or she needs only to listen without interrupting as you speak and to watch you while you act with the symbol. In my earlier story, The Demon and the Daisy, Carol didn't know she was a witness and a participant in that ceremony.

Remember you are performing the ceremony for yourself, to restore the balance in your life, to set something straight in your mind. The message is personally significant to you because it reflects a new attitude about something in your life.

If you act alone to symbolically affirm a change, tell a friend about it later. This telling creates a witness after the fact. At the very least, write about your ceremony and date it. The fun in reviewing past ceremonies is to connect the changed attitude with your present experience. It is exciting to discover the impact these simple ceremonies can have upon your life.

Ritual vs. Magic

The ritual format I use is similar to a rite of passage because it is based upon an individual's need to mark a change in attitude and/or a change in the personal experience of life. It echoes the universal theme (archetype) of death and rebirth. Using personal stories and acting with symbols, we release an old belief and affirm a new one to direct our future experience of life, restoring our sense of harmony. Unlike traditional rituals that prescribe the way participants speak and behave, my ceremonies do not repeat what has been said and done before. They change each time to reflect personal need and to permit personal expression.

Creating a personal ritual is not a way to get what we want by exerting our will upon reality. Rather than changing life, ritual can help to symbolically restore a sense of balance when we've already been changed by life. Although we cannot always control what happens to us in life, we can control our response to it.

Ritual is sacred. I always begin performing it with a reverent attitude. At the beginning of a ceremony I state its purpose and ask for the guidance and blessings of the energies of creation. All who participate combine their energies within the sacred circle of becoming, so it is appropriate to dedicate that energy in a sacred manner, affirming our individual power to transform and balance our lives. We need to be reminded that we are each an individualized aspect of Divinity experiencing physical reality. Each of us is valid in our personal expression of growth and evolving truth.

Although the effect of the ritual upon the subconscious mind can sometimes appear magical, it is not magic. Magic is a technique to alter the state of consciousness in order to facilitate psychic activity. Magical ritual is a prescribed sequence of events, chants, and statements that produce an altered state of consciousness that is directed to a desired result. Each time a magical ritual is performed it is repeated in the same manner. The intensity of concentration for the working part of the ritual requires a composed, serious attitude.[5]

The ceremonies I conduct, however, are varied and unrepetitive. They begin seriously but they are not entirely sol-

55

emn. In my opening statement I affirm that we are present to have fun and enjoy ourselves. In my eyes, a sense of humor and a tone of playfulness are also sacred. Sometimes that attitude brings us closer to the truth, permitting new insights to arise. Handling the symbol focuses the attention upon the issue it represents, but the story doesn't need to be solemn. Laughter relieves tension. Participants' stories are seldom scripted in advance. When we tell our stories about change, we are not repeating something that's already been said or established by tradition. However people choose to express themselves when it is their turn to speak is acceptable. We get more from the ceremony when we have an attitude of participatory celebration.

The Ceremony

The creation of personal ceremony adds another dimension to changing your mental programming by acting out the change with a symbol. This is your chance to speak to the subconscious mind in a symbolic manner, much as it does to you in your dreams. Invite that part of your mind to watch what you do and to listen to your story. The subconscious does not distinguish between what is real and what is vividly imagined. It takes what you firmly believe to be true as *the truth* and acts accordingly. Objectifying and acting out the change in belief through symbols of release and affirmation places the change on a physical level, where you experience life; it isn't just in your mind. By graphically acting out the change on the physical level, the mind knows exactly what you want. The change is programmed clearly, without any doubt about the desired result.

When you have determined your personal story about the change and have decided the way you will act with your symbols of change, you have the basic ingredients for a ceremony. The goal is to enact your story with full awareness and intent by performing some significant physical action with your symbols while you tell a witness your story about the change.

The following description contains suggestions to help you think about what you may want to include in your ceremony. These are only suggestions. Follow your intuition. Although this description involves a single witness, you determine the actual number to include.

Readings. Think about places within the ceremony where you can read favorite quotations, prayers, and blessings. Appendix A contains quotations and readings I've collected that I have found useful for my ceremonies. Please use them if they feel good to you.

Witness and personal symbols. Who will be with you while you act and speak? What will you wear, and what symbols of power will you have with you on the special day?

Time and place. Where will you perform the ceremony? You may want to tell your witness why this place and time for the ceremony are meaningful to you. Is there a special significance to you about the season, the month, the phase of the moon, the date, the day of the week, the time of the day? Does this date mark the passage of days, months, or years from an important event? Is it a national or religious holiday?

Marking the area. When you are at the appointed place and time you may want to define the area you've chosen to act within by sprinkling the border with a symbolic substance like cornmeal or water, or by laying out a blanket or scarf, or by making a special arrangement of furniture.

Opening. As you begin the celebration, sanctify the space and those in it with a blessing. Ask for the loving guidance and universal wisdom, the Creator, the source of all things, to be present with you and those who participate in the ceremony. Some people like to ask the blessings of the energies of the six directions (the four cardinal directions, plus above and below), and recognize themselves as individualized expressions of Divinity as the seventh direction (see "Honoring the Directions," Appendix A). You may want to symbolically purify the place and the participants with smoke, incense, or water; or the participants may symbolically cleanse themselves with water.

Intent. Make a clear focused statement describing the purpose of the ceremony. While you and your friend talk about why you are together at this place and time, you may want to light individual candles from a common flame or mutually touch a special symbol.

Personal adornment and symbols. Tell your friend about the special significance of what you're wearing. Explain what your personal symbols of power mean to you.

Story and action of change. Your story about the change provides the narrative for the ceremony and explains the significance of the symbols and actions. You may want to experiment with telling your story in the third person, as if it happened to another person in another time, or as if you were speaking for the symbol. The degree of focused intent will determine the seriousness with which your mind will accept and act upon the desired change. Release the negative feelings that have weakened you and affirm the positive beliefs that strengthen you.

You might say or think something to this effect: "This experience caused me to change my mind about myself and my experience of life. I release the pain by releasing (or transforming) this symbol. I affirm what I have gained that validates myself and my abilities by adding this symbol to my shrine of strength. I am victor, not victim!" Don't forget to mention meaningful coincidences by telling miracle stories that are connected with the events involved in the change.

Commitment to change. Will you make a commitment to the change you have described by promising to put your words into action, "walking your talk"? If you feel that an action contract (described in Appendix B) is appropriate, tell your witness what you will do within a specified time to support the desired change. You may want to symbolically affirm your pledge by shaking hands with your witness or by making a written, signed statement.

Food and friendship. Then share a small amount of food and drink with your friend to give thanks for the support of the universe and the presence of love and friendship in your life. Describe what the food and drink means to you. Symbolically affirm your feelings by making a toast, or by feeding each other a bit of food to symbolize your interdependence and interconnectedness with all of life.

Renewal. End the ceremony by symbolically centering yourself within the new reality you desire to experience. Restore your balance. You have released an old attitude and are reborn into a new way of thinking. This is a symbolic death and rebirth. You may want to affirm your new beginning and sense of harmony by standing at the center of a circle as you describe your new attitude. Or leave a mark of beauty to commemorate the change by planting seeds, flowers, a living plant, or a tree. Acting with fire, smoke, or water can affirm your renewal. Put on new shoes for the new adventures ahead of you. Share your joy with your friend by holding hands or embracing.

To symbolically affirm the recentering and renewal of my spirit, I sometimes say the Navajo Beautyway Prayer and ask my witness to scatter cornmeal around me as the directions are mentioned—"before me," "behind me," and so on. To walk in beauty is to live in harmony. The Navajo, too, realize the value of affirmative prayer!

Navajo Beautyway Prayer[6]

Today I will walk out,
Today everything evil will leave me,
I will be as I was before,
I will have a cool breeze over my body,
I will have a light body.
I will be happy forever,
Nothing will hinder me;
I walk with beauty before me,
I walk with beauty behind me,
I walk with beauty below me,
I walk with beauty above me,
I walk with beauty around me,
My words will be beautiful!

Closing. End the ceremony by making a formal declaration that you have accomplished what you set out to do and describe how you feel about it. Thank your friend for being with you at this special time. Thank the energies you honored as you began the ceremony for their participation and guidance. You may want to give your friend a token of this special time, such as a flower or an earring (see "Mementos of Friends and Events" in Chapter Two). Think of a symbolic action to end the ceremony that is the opposite of the actions you made to initiate the ceremony: if, for example, you lit candles at the opening, extinguishing them symbolically marks the closing.

Putting on a Good Show

The more senses you involve as you conduct the ceremony, the more of an impact it makes on your mind. Remember my description in Chapter One of the way the Roman Catholic Mass and a formal dinner include the senses to put on a good show. Although I have here separated the different senses to help you think about each one, it's easy to link them together.

Emotional stimulation. Get excited about the ceremony. Feel the sense of anticipation and excitement about the change you're making and the way it will affect your life. Focus on your personal sense of strength, your self-esteem, your sense of empowerment about making the change. Connect with the others present by using songs and music to evoke emotions of joy, love, and celebration.

Movement. How will you act with the symbols? Will you make meaningful, dramatic symbolic gestures with your arms and hands? How will you involve your body while acting out the change? Will you stand as you speak? How will you involve others in movement—by using circle dances, drumming, rattling, singing, chanting, clapping?

Sound. Will you use recorded or live music, songs, chants, drums, rattles, bells? The use of music connects with evoking positive emotions.

Taste. If you use special food and drink in the ceremony you may want to talk about the way it is connected to other special events, people, and places in your life. Be creative by thinking about the use of flavoring extracts, the texture of food and its visual appeal, the symbolism of taste: sweet, sour, bitter, salty.

Smell. Will you include fragrant plants or flowers, essential oils, personal fragrance, incense? Consider the aroma of the food you use in the ceremony.

Touch. The way the symbols and other objects feel can be symbolic: hard, soft, rough, spongy, spiked, furry, and so on. Experiment with the temperature of something you might handle. Think of the shape, texture, weight of symbols and food.

Sight. How will you add beauty to the environment? What images or objects of beauty, strength, and religious significance will you include? Will you have a shrine or altar? Will you use flowers? Your physical appearance is part of your personal environment and reflects your self-esteem. Explore the way you can use shapes, colors, candles, fabric, or party decorations to enhance the beauty of the setting. Think of the visual appeal of food, its arrangement and appearance.

Creating a ceremony to honor a change in your life is an opportunity for you to explore your innate creativity. It's your show! Enjoy!

NOTES

1. Richard Cavendish, editor, *Man, Myth & Magic, An Illustrated Encyclopedia of the Supernatural* (New York: Marshall Cavendish Corporation, 1970); J.E. Cirlot, *A Dictionary of Symbols* (New York: Philosophical Library, 1981); Barbara Walker, *The Woman's Dictionary of Symbols and Sacred Objects* (San Francisco: Harper & Row, 1988). I have based my list of the meanings of symbols mainly upon these works.

2. Sam Keen, *Your Mythic Journey* (Los Angeles: Jeremy P. Tarcher Inc., 1989), pp. xiv-xv.

3. Schopenhauer quoted in Joseph Campbell, *The Power of Myth* (New York: Doubleday, 1988), p. 229.

4. Joseph Campbell, *The Hero With a Thousand Faces* (Cleveland: World, 1967), pp. 245–246.

5. Richard Cavendish, editor, *Man, Myth & Magic, An Illustrated Encyclopedia of the Supernatural* (New York: Marshall Cavendish Corporation, 1970). This encyclopedia has excellent material on ritual and magic.

6. Leland C. Wyman, *Beautyway: A Navajo Ceremonial* (New York: Pantheon, 1957), pp. 141–142.

4

The Giveaway Celebration

The Giveaway is a ceremony for you and a gathering of your friends to symbolize with tangible objects the changes in your lives and your thinking that have happened and/or things you wish to experience.

Although planning ahead helps distribute the responsibility, a ceremony can be planned alone. Sometimes it's impossible to find a convenient time and place for everyone to meet to plan a ceremony. A sudden change in plans can leave you holding the bag when a participant cancels out at the last minute. Keeping things simple means keeping enough control to avoid the potential confusion when two people exchange blank stares and dismayed words like "I thought you were going to do it" when it's time to act and no one is prepared.

You can mail invitations describing the theme of the ceremony, the kind of symbol to bring, the way it will be used in the ceremony, what to wear, a dish to share after the ceremony, and so on. After reading the invitation, people have enough of an idea about the ceremony to know if it's something they want to do. As I get more ideas about what I want to include in a ceremony, I phone my friends to add to the list of things to bring. I also encourage them to share the invitation with other people they know who might enjoy participating. This allows me to meet others and make new friends, too.

It doesn't seem to matter if everyone invited to the ceremony knows each other, is within the same age group, or shares a common issue. As humans, we are all experiencing change and personal growth. Whether you plan the ceremony alone or with others who will participate in it, there are some things you need to think about ahead of time.

Plan Ahead!

In a planning session before the actual event, you and your friends will design the ceremony that will address the mutual needs and desires of the group. The ceremony centers upon the symbols of change each person has brought to give away and the stories about them. There is more energy and a genuine sense of celebration when everyone is involved with planning the event and actively participates in it. This is a celebration with spirit!

Where will the ceremony take place? Plan to begin the ceremony with a blessing of your choice. However you relate to your source, the Divinity, ask that the energy of that source be present with you and your friends, to live and move in you and through you to guide and protect you with loving wisdom. At the close of the ceremony bless and thank the energies for their participation. You may choose to mark in some sacred manner the area in which the ceremony is held, perhaps by honoring the energies of the six directions and the center. An opening meditation, prayer, song, or musical offering helps center the energies of the group. You may choose to use readings I've included in Appendix A.

What stories will the group choose to tell? To affirm the special magic happening in each person's life you may want to share "miracle stories" around the circle, whether or not the stories relate to the specific changes being addressed. You might talk about the significance of clothing or special adornment worn for the occasion. This is storytelling time! Telling these little stories before exchanging and talking about the giveaway symbols is important because the stories help your friends to know each other better and to feel they're part of the family the group represents. Storytelling transforms strangers into friends and creates a deeper sense of community.

How will the giveaway symbols be selected? Perhaps the person who initiated the idea of the ceremony will select the first object laid out on a blanket. Instead of taking turns around the circle, the first person to make a choice can pass some special symbol to any person to indicate that he or she is to choose an item next, and so on. That way, no one knows who will be next.

The major arcana of the tarot cards can be another way of determining the order of selecting the giveaway symbols. After everyone has randomly selected a card, the objects are taken according to the number on the cards. The symbolism of the cards can give each person another story to tell, freely associating with the design. Sometimes the selected card can be very meaningful to what's happening in the person's life. Did the selection occur merely by chance, or was it a meaningful coincidence?

Each person's story is special. Each person deserves the time to tell it and merits respectful attention without interruption. Depending upon the size of your group you may want to establish the maximum time a person may speak and appoint a timekeeper to remind the teller when the time is up. People lose track of time when they're caught up in telling their stories.

I've told my friends they are limited to five minutes of personal suffering—if the suffering is important to the story. This is not the moment for personal catharsis. Please encourage any friend who is having an emotionally difficult time to consult a professional therapist to help resolve the issue. One of the purposes of the Giveaway ceremony is to release resolved pain, if it exists, and to affirm the insights gained from it that support life in a positive way.

How will you symbolically affirm your renewal after the Giveaway part of the ceremony? A feast after the ceremony can be a celebration of abundance and a time to honor the food that nourishes our physical bodies and our planet, Mother Earth, which sustains all life.

The most difficult part of the planning session involves a realistic estimation of the duration of the ceremony. Leave plenty of time for the different activities, since it is distracting to have people leave before the ceremony is complete.

And finally, no matter how much advance planning is done there is almost always something unexpected that comes along. Be flexible and keep your sense of humor.

It's Celebration Time!

On the day of the ceremony, as people arrive for the Giveaway, they place their symbols on a blanket or in some designated area. If a person chooses to give away more than one object, make certain the objects from that person are grouped together. Otherwise, somebody's symbol will be left unchosen because of the confusion created when more than one person selects objects that one person brought. Some people bring their giveaway symbols wrapped as a gift. Although I prefer the gift to be visible, I have learned that it doesn't matter if the gift is concealed. It always seems to connect with the right person anyway.

If your gift is the last one chosen, please don't take it amiss; your gift was waiting for the right person to pick it up. The object's significance is not decreased because of the order in which it was selected.

After each person has selected another's object, the giver explains the significance to the recipient. By releasing the object you are marking a transition in your life and a change in your beliefs, one that you explain with your story. What has passed out of your life? What do you release? What do you affirm? How have you chosen to symbolize your transition? Telling the story and releasing your symbol graphically imprints upon your mind the change you affirm. This becomes an affirmation of your personal power, your continual blossoming and transformation as you move through life. Then end your story with an affirmation or description of what you want to experience in your life to replace what you have released.

After you have told your story about your symbol to the person who selected it, that person explains his or her object's significance to the one who picked it up. The stories zig-zag around the circle, moving from giver to taker. When the gift giver relates his or her story to the symbol, the issue is described differently from the way it would be told in normal conversation. The symbol helps to keep one's attention focused upon the issue. Setting a time limit in which to tell the story encourages brevity and conciseness.

The fun of a Giveaway ceremony is hearing others' stories, because they often strike a chord in our own hearts: we've walked that path, too. Sometimes there is a strange coincidence between the taker and the object chosen or the story told about it that addresses something very special in the taker's life.

As the giver explains the significance of the object you selected, it may remind you of similar themes in your past or present. Perhaps you're dealing with a similar issue. But it doesn't need to mean the same thing to you as it does to the giver. You had your own reason for choosing the object before you heard its story. How does the symbol speak to you? Create a story about it to affirm something positive in your life. You may already know what the object means to you, the way it connects with an inner need.

If you have difficulty relating to the object or the story, try freely associating words with it in a lighthearted manner. What other things come to you as you look at it, feel it? Its shape, size, weight, texture may provide clues as you allow your mind to resonate with it. Free association is a way to spontaneously connect to subconscious symbolism or other memories that can create a story appropriate to your situation. When you play at making up a story you move beyond your normal critical faculties to the deeper levels of the mind. Sometimes something quite profound can emerge from spontaneous free association. Relax! You can't tell a "wrong" story.

Sometimes the giver's story is not something you want to think about. Or you may have misjudged the object's appearance, thinking it was something other than what it was on closer examination. Perhaps the object is asking you to reexamine your attitude about its significance. At one Giveaway a young woman's idealism about life was challenged with the reality of life-threatening situations, like nuclear war, contained in the wrapped book she selected, *The Hundredth Monkey* by Ken Keyes Jr., a book published in 1987 by Vision Books.

By sharing your healing energies with the symbol while it is in your home, you affirm your connection with the giver and the other people who attended the ceremony. When you have enjoyed the object and are ready to release it from your environment, *please don't throw it in the trash can.* It was part of a ceremony and another person's transformation; it is sacred. It deserves to be treated with respect.

Listen to your intuition for guidance about the way to let it go. What feels right to do with it? You may want to give it to a friend to symbolize the way things come into and pass out of life. Create a story to go with it to make it more meaningful to that person, or tell how it came into your hands. Recycle it by giving it to a thrift store. Or bury it. However you choose, release the symbol with love, knowing your connection with it has been a part of the giver's personal transformation.

You may want to select a special area that appeals to the group for the blessing part of the ceremony. If you choose to use the Beautyway Prayer as the closing blessing, the taker can scatter cornmeal around the giver as the giver reads the prayer and mentions the directions ("before me," "behind me"). Even this simple gesture requires focus and intent as the blessing is spoken and the person is honored. This symbolic renewal and recentering is significant to the mind when it is done in a serious manner.

Giveaway Ceremony Suggestions

The Staff of Community

As I planned one of my Giveaway celebrations I was inspired by a vision to create a "staff of community" (see Fig. 3) to celebrate the "social security program" that my network of friends symbolized to me. As I expressed the idea to a friend, it began to take shape in his mind. He cut willow branches,

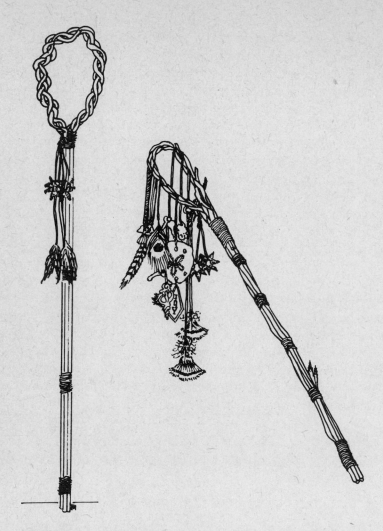

3: The Staff of Community

The staff is made of intertwined willow branches, with one end bent to form a loop. Ceremony participants decorated the loop with symbols that affirmed our interconnection with each other and our interdependence with all life.

soaked them in water, intertwined and bound them together and bent one end of the bundle into a loop. The finished product was about five feet high and looked like an armless *ankh*, the ancient Egyptian symbol of life.

I invited each of my friends to create symbols and suspend them from the circle at the top of the staff. The symbols we created from natural and found objects represented our individual spirits and honored our interconnection with life and our mutual interdependence. The decorated staff was a visual delight, a physical manifestation of our shared spirits, and the celebration of community!

When it was time to share individual stories we passed the staff of community from one person to the next. Each participant held the staff and spoke, and then passed it on to allow the next person to speak. In this way it became a "talking stick," giving the person holding it the right to speak and to be listened to with respect. Any item with special significance to the group can become a talking stick.

The Cord of Community

You may want to pass a ball of string, yarn, ribbon, or cord that is long enough to span the circumference of the circle from one person to the next at the beginning of the ceremony. As each person speaks about his or her intention, that person symbolically affirms the intention by tying a knot in the cord, passing the cord to the next person. The last person cuts the cord and ties it to form an inner circle.

In one of my ceremonies I placed a shower clip on the cord to indicate whose turn it was to speak. We joked about its being the "ring of truth." When the person was finished, the clip was passed on to the next person's knot to allow the sharing to continue.

We ended the ceremony by cutting the cord and keeping

as a memento of the ceremony the knot that each of us had tied. Another way to symbolically release the energy of the ceremony would be to burn the entire cord.

Ceremony Containers

You may wish to provide or ask the participants to bring a special object to keep with them for the duration of the ceremony. After the ceremony it becomes a memento of the special time spent together. Once I handed out small yellow foam balls to each person to absorb the energies of the ceremony. I noted with amusement that the balls gave my friends something to fidget with as they spoke and listened to others.

Blessing Buttons

A common experience in rites of passage is for the initiates to be marked in some symbolic way, such as with body designs, apparel, adornment, or a new hairstyle to affirm the change that has happened. Because the Giveaway ceremony initiates a new belief, I like to leave a symbolic mark on the participants after the closing blessing by pinning a novelty button on each person. I choose a short slogan or phrase, such as "Thank you for your heart!" or "Blossoming in Beauty," and have it commercially made into a button by a trophy business or a commercial printer. An alternative might be to hang a ribbon around the neck of each person who completes the ceremony. That's reminiscent of sports awards. We deserve a medal for our spiritual strength and courage to make a change in our lives!

Communion and the Tao

The food you share during the food and friendship part of the ceremony is another opportunity to make up a story. The following evolved as I freely associated with the concept of harmony:

To walk in beauty is to maintain a sense of harmony. The tao is a symbol of harmony because the dark and light are equally balanced. Harmony is what we are striving to achieve with ceremony, even if it addresses only a portion of our experience. We make constant adjustments in our attitude as we go along to maintain the balance between dark and light.

The circular form of the tao relates to wholeness, completion, perfection, unity. The dark and the light relate to our perception of the experiences within the circle of life. Both aspects are necessary. The seeds for growth (the small dots within the larger designs) are the lessons gleaned from what we experience subjectively.

So what's edible that is circular, with an equal amount of dark and light? What can symbolize the harmony we claim at the end of a ceremony? An Oreo Double Stuf cookie fits the need precisely. Double icing must certainly be equal to the dark cookie parts! Perhaps the dark and light symbolize the good news and the bad news.

How shall we communally eat the tao? Of course, tradition is strong to eat the icing first and the cookies last. Maybe we should go for the symbolic equal blending of the two aspects instead of eating them separately! After you've perfected the eating technique for the tao, you can move on to Mystic Mint cookies, which are more resistant to attempts to separate them from the icing.

The choices are yours because it's your story! Group participation makes it "our story"!

New-Attitude Food

Are there foods that you like today that you refused to eat at another time in your life? Since the theme of a Giveaway is transformation and change, you might like to carry it over to the food you ask your friends to bring to eat after the ceremony. Before you begin the meal ask your friends to describe the way they changed their minds about a particular food.

Giveaway Stories

The Significance of the Dragon

I began my adventures with personal storytelling by describing the symbolism of the dragon (see Fig. 4) that I brought to my first Giveaway, which I held nine months after David died. Here is the story I told:

> I am ready to release this dragon and what it symbolically represents to me.
>
> At this time in my journey I have chosen to use the dragon as a personal symbol of suffering. It appears threatening and ferocious with its fangs, claws, spiked body and pointed tail. The traditions of our society have been deeply ingrained in me. After David's transition I recognized I could no longer look to him to determine my direction in life. I am responsible for my life and creating the reality I will experience. It is time to integrate and act upon the wisdom that David and our unseen friends have shared with me. The words from one of his last channelings are significant to me: "The love, the abundance, the miracles that are your heritage should be yours. Knowing they exist and are untapped is a concept

76

4: The Dragon
*A Mexican folk art papier maché dragon is for me a personal
symbol of suffering. It appears threatening and ferocious with
its fangs, claws, spiked body, and pointed tail.*

that is very difficult for me to translate. It is as if a mother knows that a child does not respond to the love that is freely given. It is as if the father weeps because his children fail to respond to his wisdom."

As I began my transition the concept of abundance, miracles, love, and joy being my true heritage sounded like an interesting theory. I was tired of the generally accepted idea of suffering and scarcity in an uncaring world. What did I have to lose by changing my mind and accepting the more attractive philosophy of affirming abundance and miracles in the reality I would create for myself?

At first my vote for abundance was tentative. Now it is whole-hearted. I have experienced the abundance of love and miracles that you symbolize to me. I discard the idea that life is suffering and pain. I affirm that my life is filled with an abundance of love, friendship, miracles, and joy. I have been blessed with money to meet my needs and to share with others. What I have shared has been returned to me, multiplied many times again.

Farewell to "Widow"

A year later I called my friends together for another Giveaway celebration. This is the story I told at the Giveaway, using personal symbols of affirmation. Because I perceived these as symbols that affirmed myself, or represented my beliefs (see Fig. 5), they were not symbols I gave away.

I have chosen some toys to represent ideas I have about my life. They are a small plastic sword and the Care Bearfigures called Professor Cold Heart and Wish Bear.

The sword is a symbol of my inner power and

5: Widow: Symbols of Affirmation
The Care Bear figure, Wish Bear, represents the power of visualization and affirmation. The sword is a symbol of my inner power and strength. Another Care Bear figure, Professor Cold Heart, represents people who act in cruel, uncaring ways.

strength, a symbol that has been a recurring image in my waking dreams. I place my security within myself instead of in the outer reality. I trust the innate wisdom, courage, and safety of my spirit.

To me, Wish Bear is symbolic of the power of visualization and affirmations that are the magic of manifestation. I affirm the magic in my life. The closed eyes of the bear convey inner vision to me. I affirm that the right circumstances will be presented to me so that I can accomplish my goals and allow the miracles to manifest. May I have the wisdom to discriminate between letting go and taking control. I choose to believe that the lamp cradled in Wish Bear's arms is a symbol of the genies who are the source of my inner guidance.

Professor Cold Heart represents for me the specter of the "cold, cruel world." To me he symbolizes the chill that envelops me when I weaken and allow fear and panic to run rampant through my mind. I thought it would be good for me to have a visual symbol of a fear that I am trying to release. May peace replace the panic. May I cherish and love myself more as I fear less.

This I Release

My giveaway is the title of *widow*, symbolized by the lace handkerchief (see Fig. 6). I have hidden behind the title and played the role so well! "Oh woe is me! What is to become of the poor little widow woman?" the widow cries, wringing her hands and dabbing her eyes with her handkerchief.

Even on a humorous level, this is a story I'm telling myself. The story I tell myself is the life I bring forth. I can no longer afford to play with this title, used in the melodramatic form, because it denotes a woman who is powerless to prevent the mortgage collector from foreclosing on her home. Eventually, against impossible odds,

6: Widow: Symbols of Release
A substitute symbol for a chambered nautilus, the pointed spiraled shell represents the spiral nature of personal growth. The lace handkerchief, a melodrama prop, is a symbol for a widow. The feather tied below the handkerchief stands for an answered prayer. The image of a meadow on the novelty button symbolizes a place of inner peace.

the widow in the melodrama is saved by the hero or heroine and lives happily ever after.

In this day of personal empowerment I recognize that the savior has got to be myself. I firmly claim my power and my unlimited creative abilities to find solutions to the challenges I face. I am responsible for my life and for creating my reality. The wailing, whimpering, wallowing widow is no more, and I celebrate her transformation! I am victor, not victim!

I continue to affirm that this is a warm, kind world. My life is filled with the love of my friends, who have helped me in numerous ways. I have touched the lives of others and helped them however I could. In this way I have given back what I have received from those who have reached out to me. This is the ripple effect as I joyfully share what I can of myself. This woman is no island!

My vote is for the power of visualization and affirmations to manifest my desires. The image on the novelty button of a meadow with a rainbow over it is the place of peace I visualize when I meditate. The giveaway of the money is my affirmation of financial abundance. I am casting my lot for the magic of abundance and miracles that exist in the face of apparent scarcity.

The feather tied to the handkerchief represents a prayer I made at a friend's request. I know in some small way my love joined that of others to help resolve the problem harmoniously. As part of the giveaway, the feather affirms the power of my loving energies.

(I didn't have a chambered nautilus [see Fig. 7] to illustrate the following point, so I used another shell that grew in a spiral as a substitute symbol for the nautilus shell.)

The pointed spiral shell symbolizes a chambered nautilus, which grows in a spiral, periodically erecting partitions as it expands. The last opening is the most

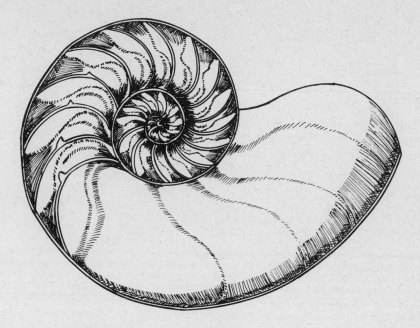

7: The Chambered Nautilus
This shell is a symbol of personal growth and evolution.

expansive one. This represents the growth potential constantly present for each of us. Let us always move forward and push past those limitations that would restrict our growth.

Visualize a small opening in the center of each partition of the nautilus. Then imagine a thread that runs from the point of the spiral through each partition opening and attaches to the animal form that has created the shell. This is the spirit line that can draw from the wisdom of the past as it steadily grows toward the future. Like the nautilus, I have symbolically erected a partition to mark the beginning of a new growth period.

5
Stories, Symbols, Action—and Creativity!

Stories I Tell Myself

Living alone without David to tell me I was loved made it painfully obvious that no matter what happened in my life, I was my only constant companion. I began to make friends with myself by creating stories that affirmed my abilities and my situation. When I attached a story to a physical object, the symbol then reflected the story back to me each time I looked at it. Symbols I selected contained the stories that helped to give my life the meaning I needed and added sparkle to my spirit.

Personal symbols are aspects of the larger story I tell myself. When I wear my phoenix earrings (see Fig. 8), they reflect the story that affirms my ability to survive crisis and to use it for growth. The fabric butterfly (see Fig. 9) affirms the pleasures and new talents I've discovered as I've learned to enjoy my different lifestyle.

8: The Phoenix Earrings

These earrings are symbolic of my ability to survive crisis and to use it for positive growth. The phoenix is a classical symbol of rebirth or renewal after apparent destruction.

Changing My Mind

Paying attention to my mental self-talk, I began to identify dispiriting theories about life that surfaced when I despaired about my situation. If words have power and I was creating my own reality, I could not allow the stories to deny who I was or what I could do or experience. To redirect my attitude, I created a new story to replace the nonproductive one, using anything that came to mind that empowered me.

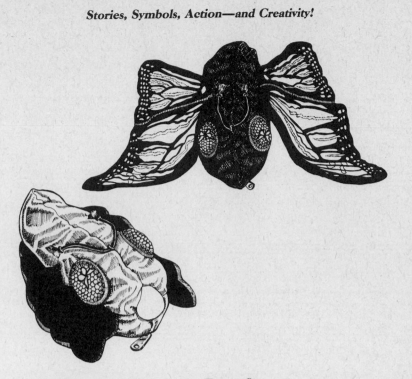

9: The Caterpillar and the Butterfly

The caterpillar represents self-limiting beliefs and resistance to transformation. Through a zipper in its belly the caterpillar can be turned inside out to become an emergent butterfly, which affirms the pleasures and new talents I've discovered as I've learned to enjoy my different lifestyle.

Symbols as Story Phrases

Combining different symbols can represent words in an affirmation. To honor and affirm the presence of financial abundance in my life I decided to place a check from a painting sale in the "cup of abundance." I set the cup on the blessing basket I use to scatter cornmeal. As a final touch I placed the joyful

Buddha figure next to it (see Fig. 10). The arrangement of these symbols on my dining room table expressed my gratitude to the abundant universe for its blessings in my life. "My life is rich, abundant, and joyful!" I affirmed to myself. It is important to affirm what is present in life (in this case, money) as much as it is to affirm what has not yet materialized. After my mind had absorbed and celebrated the message the arrangement of symbols represented, I deposited the check. When I can't delay cashing a check but still want to celebrate a sale, I place the deposit receipt instead of the check in the tin cup.

Re-Spiriting Old Symbols

A symbol that has lost its significance or reflects something no longer meaningful can be given a new spirit with another story. The wedding belt that symbolized my marriage to David (see Fig. 11) now reflects my broader commitment to celebrate my friends and my life.

Giving Stories with Gifts

When I realized how stories gave my spirit a boost, I began creating stories to go with the gifts I gave to others. While gift-wrapping creates eye appeal, a special story creates mind appeal. With the right story, ordinary objects can become special because the story has made it significant to the recipient.

10: "My Life is Rich, Abundant, and Joyful!"
Symbols of affirmation are linked to form the sentence, "My life is rich, abundant, and joyful!" The tin cup of abundance is filled with money and placed upon a basket to symbolize a blessing. The Buddha figure with upraised arms relates to joy.

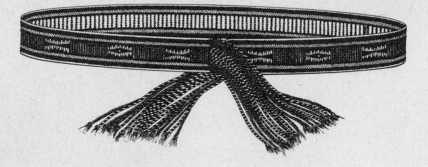

11: The Wedding Belt
The belt symbolizes the transformation of my marriage into a broader commitment to celebrate my friends and my life.

Miracle Stories

When my needs are met in unexpected ways I document these surprises by writing down the "miracle stories" to impress them upon my memory. Stringing these stories together, I have created a "trail of trust" that affirms the presence of unseen guidance and shows me the way events in life are right on schedule. The history of past miracle stories helps me keep the faith when I'm feeling uncertain about the future.

Even if these miracles are simple coincidences, my attitude about these events contributes to the celebration of life. After I wrote "Spider at My Door," a story you'll read below, I remembered that a year before I had given away spider web-shaped earrings in two Giveaways. Now I had the genuine thing in my life as an additional affirmation!

Mental Fitness is Flexibility

When your life changes, change the story you tell yourself. Personal storytelling restores the spirit and helps you remain flexible and positive in times of change. When your spirit loses its sparkle, polish it up with a new story!

> Love is the source,
> Joy is the power,
> Life is the celebration!

Symbols of Affirmation

The Phoenix Earrings

The phoenix earrings (see Fig. 8) were given to me on the day of Christmas Eve when David's body was cremated. Because of the day's events my mind told me it was a phoenix symbol, although other people may have seen a dove. Then it was simple for my mind to create the first story of affirmation for myself because, to me, the phoenix symbolized new life arising from the ashes of what had been burned away—new beginnings!

This is It!

> Participating in David's shamanic workshops
> I danced with my demon,
> fruitlessly trying to make peace with my
> fear of David's death
> at some unknown future time.
> How could I live without my husband?
> "Someday it will come," I told myself.
> "Please let it be very far away.
> There are many things
> David needs to share first."

Suddenly
I am confronted by the reality of the event
I had feared for so long.
"No!" I scream,
clawing at the nothingness
where there used to be substance,
my chest a gaping wound
where my heart has been ripped out.
An icy cold grips my aching spirit.
There is no warmth.
I am sleeping with pillows
piled on the empty side of the bed,
an illusion of what used to be solid.
Sedatives give way to wine
as I besot myself into a stupor to prevent
waking before morning,
fearing the loneliness of night,
the drunken monkey mind chanting,
"David is dead."
It can't be!

Knowing that although his body is dead,
his spirit is very much alive,
I laugh at the paradox of life in death,
the unreality of the nightmare.
Seeing the body without the spirit— this is
death.
This is the unreal reality.
The door of the cremation oven
slides shut with the finality of death.
When one door closes
another one opens.
Life loses its color.
Food loses its taste.

All is rendered to dust.
The sterile cremains
delivered in a plain brown box—
this is how it ends.
A gift of phoenix earrings:
hope,
life out of the ashes,
new beginnings.

Symbols of Affirmation

The Caterpillar and the Butterfly

Shortly after David's death a friend gave me a fabric butterfly
(see Fig. 9) as a visual symbol of my transformed life.
Through a zipper in its belly the butterfly could be turned
inside out to become a caterpillar. A physical action transformed it from one state to the other. At that point in my
transition I didn't feel like a butterfly. Sitting alone with it,
I turned it inside out and zipped it up again so that the butterfly was concealed within the caterpillar. I left it sitting on
the back of the couch to notice when I passed by it.

For a long time I felt like a caterpillar, although I had to
admit my life had changed. Certainly, my experience of life
was different, much as a butterfly's life contrasts with its previous caterpillar state.

I began to handle and play with the caterpillar/butterfly,
using it to reflect the fluctuations in my attitude between
despair and optimism. On good days the butterfly would affirm
life. When I felt despondent I identified with the caterpillar.
There were times when these silent companions, "Whoo-
pee!" and "Poor Me," transformed back and forth many times
during a single day. In some strange way I found it comforting

to symbolically act upon my feelings as I manipulated the object's appearance to conform with my state of mind. Eventually, I saw more of the butterfly and less of the caterpillar.

"Out there" in the natural world of butterflies and caterpillars, butterflies probably have little interest in reverting to caterpillars. Butterflies don't mourn what they were because they specialize in being what they are now: butterflies, not caterpillars!

Symbols of Affirmation—New Stories for Old Ones

The Wedding Vase and the Spirit Bowl

Although we never owned one, I symbolized the life I shared with David by an Indian wedding vase, which has two long necks opening into a common bowl (see Fig. 12). Blending our energies into this vase, filling it with our creative responses and love, we moved through life, sharing that love by reaching out to others we met. In a sense, we filled and drank from the vase, always supporting and loving each other, celebrating the incredible richness of our union.

With David's death the vase was smashed to dust in my mind's eye. The dream was dead. The spiritual richness had vanished. I was alone. The support and unconditional love I had known was gone. My life felt like dust. As I disposed of David's belongings I saw myself in my mind sweeping up the pieces of that vase, sweeping up the dust that symbolized my new reality.

An alarm bell rang in the back of my mind. I was affirming my life to be dust, and that wasn't healthy. So I put my mind to work creating a new symbol and story to tell myself. I asked my inner friend for guidance and wrote down the response that came to my mind:

12: The Wedding Vase and the Spirit Bowl

The wedding vase on the left with two necks is a Southwestern Indian symbol for marriage. I used the fetish bowl on the right to stand for the transformation of my status from being married to being single. It affirms an open exchange of love and friendship with others in my life instead of directing my attention to a single individual. The little carved animals (Indian fetishes) shown here are kept inside the bowl and represent my personal strengths.

"Look where you've avoided looking—to the beauty of your own spirit. There is a way to transform the pain. Take the dust, mix it with your tears, mold it into clay, and form it into a bowl. Now you have a spirit bowl. Fill it with the magic of your spirit. As an open bowl, the contents are present to nourish those who may need it. Do not deny others the richness of your spirit. Do not deny yourself the richness others can contribute to your life. This is the path with heart. Nothing is ever lost; it is only transformed!"

Some time later the same friend who had given me the phoenix earrings gave me a small Southwest fetish bowl, decorated with turquoise chips and feathers and containing within it two tiny fetishes. My mind immediately recognized it as the spirit bowl. With that awareness, I laughed and told her how perfectly the bowl symbolized the new spirit of my life!

Symbols of Affirmation—New Stories for Old Ones

The Wedding Belt

The night we were married, David had given me a hand-woven Pueblo Indian wedding belt (see Fig. 11), explaining that the white designs against the red background represented us as individuals and as a unit. The two horizontal Vs with their points meeting (><) symbolized our individual spirits; the Vs pointing away from each other (<>) creating an enclosure for a white dot at the center symbolized the fruits of our combined efforts.

After David's death the wedding belt silently taunted me as a symbol of a relationship that was gone, a symbolic death certificate hanging on the bedroom wall. Time passed. I worked through the grief, learning to accept the finality of

David's death. Now I was surviving on my own, living without him.

One day I took the belt off the wall, shook off the dust, and tied its six-foot length around my waist—something I had never done during our marriage. It complemented my casual wardrobe, a touch of the Southwest with the fringed ends dangling to the bottom of my black skirt.

What new positive story could I tell myself that would affirm my single status? The old story focused upon something that was gone. What did I have now? I had friends who accepted me for who I was. They had fed my spirit in numerous ways, supplying what I used to receive from David, although not in the same way. Thinking about this, I decided that one V represented myself while the other represented the people who were significant to me, weaving new strands of beauty into my life. The symbolic seed was the love created from my interaction with them. Wearing the belt around my waist at the center of my body affirmed the sense of centeredness and interconnectedness I was creating by myself.

This new story has given me a feeling of strength each time I wear the belt or notice it hanging on my wall. I'm glad I changed my belt's story!

Symbols of Affirmation—New Stories for Old Ones

The Tin Cup of Abundance

I have learned to pay attention to the words that slip from my mouth in casual conversation with my friends. I noticed that when we discussed our financial situations I would joke that I hadn't yet been forced to sit on a street corner and beg for money with a tin cup. The more I listened to myself the more I heard "tin cup."

Reflecting upon the phrase and the way I used it made it obvious to me that I was denying abundance by affirming scarcity. This was a story I was telling myself. Did I want to experience it? If I didn't, it was time to change my story.

Wandering down the aisles of a variety store one day I found a display of tin cups. Next to them at a higher price were enameled white cups with flower decals. I selected the high-class version of the tin cup (see Fig. 13). I was changing my story from poverty to abundance, so this was no time to pinch pennies! I placed the enameled cup on my desk so that I would notice it while I considered my next step.

A few weeks later a friend asked me to go with her to a

13: The Tin Cup of Abundance
The cup symbolizes an affirmation of financial abundance to replace a former attitude of insufficiency.

spring in the mountains to collect drinking water. On a whim, I grabbed the cup as we headed out the door.

I'd never been to the spring before. The water, instead of bubbling up from the ground as I had fantasized, gushed through a metal pipe. But I had to admit that using the pipe was a more practical way to fill jugs.

I noticed with fascination how the stream of water poured from the pipe, ebbing and flowing with its own pulse, making us work a little harder as we tried to position the jugs to catch the water. Observing this, I thought of the blood that pulsed through my body. Here was an equally vital fluid pulsing from the body of Mother Earth.

I asked my friend to witness the words and actions of an impromptu ceremony that had just come to me. Taking my tin cup, I allowed the water to pour into it, filling and spilling out of it. "I am grateful for this abundant gift from Mother Earth," I said. "This is the symbolic gift of life, unconditional love, and abundance. Scarcity is an illusion created by fear. I release that illusion from my life. With this cup I affirm the flow of financial abundance into my life."

"I'll drink to that!" my friend exclaimed with delight. Together, we affirmed abundance in our lives by sipping from the communion chalice of abundance, the tin cup.

The action and the words symbolically transformed the tin cup of poverty into one of abundance. After this ceremony the "tin cup of scarcity" disappeared from my vocabulary. Now, each time I notice it on my desk, the cup is a visual symbol of the abundance and richness in my life.

An Affirmation Becomes Reality

The Nest and the Fledgling

After David died, I found the following poem that he had written. I think it was inspired by a previous heart attack, one that he had experienced twelve years earlier. This was a story he told himself to reflect his relationship with me.

The Fledgling

Dancing,
I glanced up and saw you,
frightened, a fledgling,
struggling to raise your wings,
to fly and soar into your own space.
I tried to fan away your fear,
to lift away the weight of my love that
pinned you to the nest.
And yet your fear held you down.
Your dreams of flying were
buried beneath my weight.
I knew that if you were to fly
I would have to find another space.
To free your wings, the nest must fall.
Now an empty nest stares back at me.
My dance is almost done except for
one last soaring sweep through the
windways of my dreams.
—David Paladin

When David died my level of joy in life was drastically diminished. I had been humbled and brought to my knees, stripped of the love I had known. I felt alien and alone, an outsider looking at life rather than one who fully participated in it.

I didn't feel bitter that the joy was diminished, but I did wonder if the same feeling would ever be present for me with the intensity that I had known in my "other life." So I began to observe the mystery of life around me and to notice joy in other places outside myself. Puppies and babies became symbolic affirmations of joy. Perhaps I was trying to call my spirit back when it had retreated from life.

I knew how fleeting life was and how time changed experience; each moment was precious and irretrievable as it flowed past me. I hoped others would not have to experience loss to recognize what was present for them to enjoy in the present moment.

So my challenge was to find some way of evoking the joy from within myself, a way that was independent of outside stimulus. How could I become my own source of joy, having experienced it only when I interacted with something or someone else? Was it possible to generate the feeling by myself?

All of this I filed away in my mind, programming it with affirmations that directed myself to recognize joy around me as I lived my life. I felt joy that others who believed in me and believed in David's art and his philosophy were present to meet my needs, so I saw that I was not alone with the challenges I faced. Perhaps a better name for this feeling, as I described it, was gratitude.

One of the things I enjoyed the most during my time with David was wondering about things and philosophizing. I have an insatiable curiosity, and I love to learn.

Sharing my curiosity, David drew from a variety of adventures in his past with other native tribes that had introduced him to the shamanic practice of "talking with the ancestors"—channeling wisdom from those who are no longer physical. This practice allowed him to grow past the Navajo taboo against associating with the dead, to develop his channeling ability, to address our mutual interests. Over time, he also developed the ability to communicate and channel other shamans who were living.

One day as I reviewed material for a writing project, I found a transcript of a conversation I'd had with Umik, an Eskimo shaman who channeled through David. In this conversation Umik explained that as shaman to his tribe he helps his people understand why mysterious events have happened, individually or tribally. Then he went on to say that he believed it was important to prescribe some physical action to help his people restore their sense of harmony with the tribe and the environment. "Most good shamans try to give their people power to do something," Umik stated. "When you get the people to act in some way themselves, to do something, the healing works better, whether it's mind or body. Things work better that way. Got to get them to do something, anything." Physical action, he said, is therapeutic because it empowers the person to set things right, to restore balance to life. Symbolic action "helps make the healing work better."

Up to that point, everything I had been doing for my own healing had been with my mind as I carefully crafted positive stories. Until then, the need to act upon the stories to help the "healing" work better had not occurred to me. Using a symbol to act with (or upon) naturally followed from that idea. Acting with symbols and explaining their significance created a personal ceremony. Suddenly it became so clear and simple to me that I laughed aloud.

Here was the proverbial "Aha" experience! Laughing at this revelation, I began to dance around the room. The joy began to manifest, my breathing deepened, my chest rose and fell—in sharp contrast to my typical shallow breathing. As I noticed the rhythm of my rising and falling chest I thought of a bird flying high and free, with its wings beating effortlessly as it soared through the sky.

Then I remembered the nest that David had written about

in his poem, "The Fledgling." The nest had indeed fallen! I had no need for it any longer. I had "hatched" my first truly inspiring idea. The joy I felt came from myself. I was soaring free, high and proud, independent of outside stimulus.

Because I had programmed my mind to notice joy when it was present I recognized instantly what I was feeling and knew I needed to honor this inspiration as a positive element of my growth. What did I need for celebrating this joy?

I wanted a nest to acknowledge the fulfillment of David's prophecy in "The Fledgling." A local hobby store had a display of handcrafted nests (see Fig. 14). I selected one woven of plant material with numerous downy seeds. Next to the nest section were plastic bags filled with tiny eggs the size of pea gravel. They were much too small for the nest, but they were the only ones available. I chose to purchase them because I intuitively felt this nest needed eggs in it.

I visited a toy store to locate a bird for my nest. David didn't indicate what kind of bird this fledgling was, but I knew I wanted an eagle, because eagles are strong, powerful birds. Nothing but the strongest of birds would suffice for this graphic symbol to my mind!

Alas, toy eagles are not in plentiful supply. After several blank looks from salespeople when I asked them if they had anything in stock that would address my need, the store manager directed me to a collection of plastic male dolls packaged with winged mascots depicting a variety of strengths. A doll named SteelWill came with what looked like a blue plastic eagle named StrongHold.[1] Chuckling to myself, I said, "I'll buy that!" and left the store with my purchase, feeling triumphant in my quest.

As I sat at the table with my trophies assembled before me, a story began to form in my mind that related to them. The nest symbolizing my life with David had fallen. Now I was standing as tall and feeling as strong alone as I had felt before,

14: The Nest and the Fledgling

The nest is symbolic of incubation, and the eggs represent unexplored potentials. The primitive doll relates to shamanic qualities I admire. The eagle is a symbol for spiritual strength and flight, while the ring with its tiny arrowhead stands for life purpose and direction. A bit of snakeskin in the nest represents rebirth and transformation. Pokey, the pony, symbolizes wisdom.

when David was with me. A part of my spirit that had for so long been depressed was finally restored to its fullness.

A nest is symbolic of incubation. This was *my* nest now, a symbol of what I was incubating within myself. I decided the tiny eggs symbolized the creative potential that was yet to be explored but would "hatch" at appropriate times in my life to manifest the path with heart that I longed to experience.

Eggs need something to sit on them. As I searched my home for what would symbolically incubate the eggs, I found a primitive bone doll, which I had always thought of as a shaman. The shaman doll is a single piece of bone about three inches long with a crudely carved face depicting eyes, nose, and mouth. Attached by sinew through holes at the top and bottom of the body are oversized arms and hands and small legs, fashioned out of a similar bone, bisected.

Placing the shaman on top of the eggs in the nest, I acknowledged that I had some qualities similar to a shaman's. Because the shaman figure sat within the nest, it signified that the qualities I admired were also being incubated within myself, in the process of becoming.

I clipped the eagle onto the side of the nest, the source of its birthplace, although the eagle was no longer restricted to it. Its powerful wings were raised in flight, symbolic of my spiritual flight. Thinking about its blue color brought a smile as I wondered if it was the "blue bird of happiness."

I also chose to deposit within the nest other things I wanted to incubate: a ring with an arrowhead, symbolic of my purpose and direction; a green crystal, symbolic of abundance to support my creative explorations; a bit of snake skin, representing rebirth and transformation. I placed my orange pony, Pokey, so that its head looked over the edge of the nest. I'd found another pony!

My trophy honoring my growth was complete. It was a symbol of transition that I chose to keep on my dining table, a place of high visibility, to affirm my growth symbolically every time I looked at it.

Occasionally I added or removed objects from the nest as my needs dictated, and I placed the pony in different positions. By combining different symbols and changing the arrangement of the objects, I changed the story I told myself and renewed my conscious awareness of the nest and its contents. The nest became a microcosm for the macrocosm of my physical reality.

Now I know it is possible for me to feel joy within myself. Others may augment that joy, but I'm no longer dependent upon outside sources to experience it. My story has changed. The nest is symbolic of that transition. I honor myself and my growth.

Gifts with Stories

The Tear of Joy

A friend encouraged me to call her friend, Batya, while I was in Denver. Although I didn't know Batya, I believed in the power of networking and was always open to the adventures it offered.

I warmed to Batya right away; she felt like "family" to me, and I was glad I'd called. As we got to know each other I recounted a little of my past, mentioning the loss of my husband and my resultant grief. Because she was such an attentive listener I went on to tell her the way I used symbols and created stories to make the gifts I gave to others more meaningful to them.

Batya told me she'd attended a gem show earlier in the day. She had spent a great deal of time selecting a light turquoise blue topaz cut in a teardrop shape (see Fig. 15), which she had no use for herself. She didn't know why she needed to buy it, but she trusted her intuition and brought it home. As she finished recounting the day's adventures, her face lit up and she brought out the topaz. "Now I know why I bought this stone!" she exclaimed.

Anticipating what was coming, my hands slammed shut.

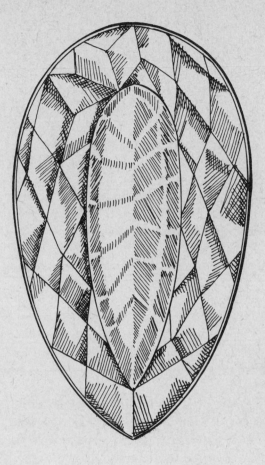

15: The Tear of Joy
This turquoise blue topaz, which came with a story from a friend, is a gift affirming the future experience of great joy in my life.

After prying them apart and admonishing me to receive gifts graciously, Batya placed the gem in my then-open palm.

"Okay, now tell me a story about it," I challenged her. Catching on to the game, she thought a moment and then said, "This is a tear of joy. Tears of grief are dark gray. I know you're familiar with them. This blue tear is symbolic of tears of joy that will come to you in the future!"

I liked that story and have treasured the stone because of what it symbolizes to me. It makes me feel good to affirm that at some future time I will experience joy so intensely that I will be moved to tears. It is an excellent healing story that nurtures my spirit in a very special way!

Later, when I heard that my book about ceremonies would be published, I wrote to Batya to tell her the joyful news and the way I had decided to use the "tear of joy." Since my philosophy is now to invest in myself, the tear of joy will be set in a ring for me to symbolize the joy of seeing the book in print.

Gifts with Stories

The Gold Star Award

While I was visiting with a friend in another city, we went to a restaurant that served, among other things, soup and cornbread. I selected the soup, serving myself at the soup and salad bar, and returned to the table. Then I remembered that cornbread went with it, but I didn't know where to find it.

A waitress some distance from me, not assigned to wait on my table, noticed the puzzlement written on my face. She asked if she could get me something. I burst out laughing as I thought how I must have looked for her to read me so easily.

She came over to the table while I was still laughing. I told her how much I appreciated her ability to recognize my confusion. Her concern was so genuine that I reached out and hugged her. After more chatting and laughing we finally got around to what had initiated our exchange. She brought the cornbread to me instead of telling me where to find it myself.

I was so impressed with her motherly concern I wanted to appreciate her in a symbolic way. Later when she returned to the table I handed her a five-dollar bill wrapped around my business card.

"You do so well addressing other people's needs that I'm guessing you seldom do special things for yourself." She admitted that was true. "This is a symbolic gold star from me to you to show you how much I appreciate your sensitivity to my needs. I want you to spend this money on something that is for your own personal pleasure. You deserve something nice for yourself that you wouldn't otherwise have."

She promised she would do so. I don't know if she actually followed through or not. That doesn't matter. More important was the fact that I appreciated her and encouraged her to do something nice for herself, and that she had a symbol to take home with her to remind her of our meeting.

Grinning, I told my friend that I enjoyed the creative challenge of using what is present to address a need when it arises. Special stories can make any object more meaningful. This episode affirmed my ability to add sparkle to another's life with a simple symbolic gesture. My spirit was brightened because I had touched a stranger in a special way.

When I appreciate others I delight in their surprised responses, especially when they realize there are no hidden, selfish motives on my part. I know I remain in their memory longer than those who have verbally abused them. Appreciation doesn't cost a thing, and it makes both of us feel good! Home-made cookies are my traditional symbol of appreciation.

A gift of appreciation symbolically affirms and connects me to the goodness in other people. For me, acting this way wherever I am, whenever I feel it, is the kind of symbolic affirmation that contributes to the greater healing of the planet. There is something I can do to heal "in my own back yard." I use affirmations to nourish my spirit and appreciation to nourish others' spirits. Appreciation affirms life and multiplies the joy.

If energy follows thought, I prefer to attract acts of kindness. By recognizing and honoring basic human goodness, I find that it manifests in my life on a regular basis in miraculous ways.

Gifts with Stories

The Heroine and the Crone

A friend from Kansas came to visit me on her way to the Zuñi Reservation. During the course of our leisurely visit over a meal she told me about a series of coincidences that had created in her heart a strong desire to visit the Zuñi Indians. Two months ago she didn't even know they existed!

I could immediately relate her dream to the theme of a hero's quest—an archetype I had been reading about in Joseph Campbell's *The Power of Myth*,[2] supplemented by videotapes of the Bill Moyers/Joseph Campbell interviews aired by the local Public Broadcasting Station.[3] I smiled at the coincidence of a heroine on her quest manifesting at the same time I was studying the theme.

When she was ready to leave on the final leg of her journey she hesitated. She expressed her fears to me. "Am I doing the right thing? Maybe this is just a crazy idea I've imagined in my mind. Maybe there is nothing there for me. Maybe I shouldn't go." There were so many unknowns. There was no certainty.

Here was my chance to be the wisdom figure (in this case, the crone) every heroine needs when she's feeling faint-hearted. I searched my "cottage" for some magic to give her faith and courage to stay with the quest.

I sat her down and paraphrased from Campbell. "The most important thing you must do is to be true to your heart and to follow your bliss. Take heart and encouragement from me when it is lacking in yourself." To symbolize my faith in her vision I handed her a red paper heart (see Fig. 16). "And if you don't follow your bliss this is what you'll become." I gave her a piece of petrified wood (also in Fig. 16).

16: Gifts for the Heroine
The paper heart is a gift I gave to encourage a friend who was on a quest. I also gave her the piece of petrified wood to remind her that there is no growth without risk.

As she examined the wood, some pieces flaked off in her hand. She quipped, "You mean if I don't follow my bliss, I'll become a flake!" She'd gotten the point.

I gave her a hug and told her, "If you begin to feel faint-hearted, remember the symbols and what they mean. You've got some magic, and I know you'll have a great adventure!"

She left, encouraged and enheartened, with her magic symbols to remind her of the message from the "wise old woman who lived in a magical cottage near the mountain."

A few weeks later, the heroine called me to tell me about the success of her quest and to thank me for my magic when she needed it the most. If she had turned back, she would never have had the honor of attending a private ceremony or meeting the wonderful Zuñi Indians who so graciously took her into their home and made her welcome.

"Sure, Lady," I replied. "It was my pleasure. Thanks for allowing me to be part of your magical quest!"

Miracle Stories

Divine Magic in Daily Life

As I have become aware of the strange way my needs are met I am increasingly convinced that an invisible helping hand is operating in my life. Sometimes when I'm uncertain about the way to satisfy a pressing need in my mind, a friend will mention in conversation that she has heard of a place or person that may meet that need, either before or after I'm aware of the need. Eventually, my mind "clicks" as it connects resource and need. Then I set off to explore the potential. Usually, the outcome exceeds my anticipation. "Here is what I've been looking for, and more!" I exclaim delightedly to myself. With a sigh of relief, I praise that helping hand for directing me. And I praise myself for being open to its guidance.

This web of connections helps affirm an unseen interconnection between my life and those of others, and it helps explain the more peculiar ways my needs are met. Much of my success with problem-solving has been through brain-picking and networking. Although I take full responsibility for the outcome, I seldom act without another's counsel, information, or reference.

There is no way I can logically explain these miracles in my life, so I've had to disengage my analytical mind from trying to do it. But that's all right. Instead, I use the miracles to show me that I'm on track; I'm where I need to be.

With this attitude things seem to flow easily, effortlessly, facilitating the perfect unfolding of my life. No longer do I feel the need to control my life with a clenched fist or believe that I'm alone in an uncaring world. Relaxing, knowing my needs will be met, I have fallen into the invisible support that is omnipresent.

Even failures can be miracles. Sometimes opportunities come along that appear to be sound. I pursue them. They flop. The energy disappears as fast as it came. A project doesn't pan out. Is this failure?

I don't think so. Given some time to reflect upon the people involved and the failed outcome, I can see where the idea wasn't as sound or the people weren't as dependable or motivated as I had believed earlier. When nothing seems to be working I back off from the project, assuming it may not be appropriate for me to pursue it. It would be foolish to try to make something work through sheer force of will.

For me, some "failures" point to the unseen guidance that knows what is better for me than I do. The underlying reality beneath the illusion may be hazardous to my health. Paying attention to this wisdom, I've felt invisibly protected. My openness and desire to trust life remains intact because events that may have destroyed those qualities have been kept from me. That's the story I tell myself. Failure may be only "a blessing in disguise," another miracle to observe as I affirm the greater wisdom and bless it for its loving protection.

I say to myself, "Divinity exists within me. I rely upon it, I trust it, I submit to its wisdom. I joyously give myself whole-heartedly and unreservedly to the Divinity that guides my creative expression and bestows meaning upon my life." Affirmations keep my mind open to the love, guidance, and protection that surround me. Along with suffering, I've given up failure!

The more I pay attention to the events in my life, the "failures," and the way my needs are met, the more strongly I believe in miracles. With this increased awareness the experience of joy, love, and awe has become so intense at times that daily experience can take on a religious feeling. The Divinity has become alive, sparkling through myself, my activities, and those whom I meet!

It is not unusual for me to affirm those who warm my heart by telling them they are miracles in my life. They may not understand what I mean, but they know it's a compliment and smile with surprise.

A Miracle Story

"Firey"

It didn't take me long to recognize how much my audience enjoyed the symbols I used to illustrate the concepts I explained in my presentations about personal ceremony. Burdened with symbols as I entered the meeting room, I would grin, thinking about the strange array of items that were the tools of my trade.

As the concepts for my presentations evolved I decided I needed a symbol to illustrate graphically how an event can figuratively dismember us because of the attendant beliefs and fears that surface automatically in our consciousness when we face the unknown. Searching my memory for something to address that need, I remembered seeing a friend's daughter deftly remove a doll's legs to more easily dress it.

During an out-of-town speaking engagement I entered a toy store and asked a sales clerk if he had dolls whose arms and legs could be removed. He looked at me with some consternation, denying that there was such a thing. Obviously, he had never experienced the challenge of dressing dolls. I could imagine the thoughts my request evoked in his mind. I was probably some sadistic woman who pulled wings off butterflies!

As he gave my request more thought, his face lit up. "Maybe you'd be interested in a stuffed creature I'm always reassembling. We've had it in the store for a long time. Poor thing has had a rough time, because the kids are always pulling his arms, legs, and head off, and it takes me some searching to locate all the missing parts to put him back together again. I haven't been able to sell him. If you're interested, you can have him for half price."

I was curious and believed in keeping my options open. "Show me what it looks like and I'll tell you if I'm interested."

He produced a strange-looking pink doll (see Fig. 17) that had long pointed ears and a conical nose. Its protruding eyes had red pupils outlined in yellow against a blue circle ringed with green and yellow. Red fake fur at the shoulders and hips disguised the hook-and-loop fasteners for the arms, head, and legs. The only permanently attached appendage was its tail, affixed below and behind its wrinkled mid-

17: "Firey"

The toy is a symbol for the sense of psychological dismemberment experienced in a crisis.

section. The tag that accompanied this critter indicated that "he" was "Firey," a character from the movie, "Labyrinth."[4]

I didn't hesitate a second. Here was something that more perfectly addressed my need than I could have imagined. The expression on Firey's face was irresistible: it was a classic illustration of a transition and the way it alters our state of consciousness, symbolized in his eyes. His wry smile is almost imperceptible. This critter is a survivor; dismemberment doesn't threaten him in the least.

Although he is a perfect transition symbol, Firey is also a symbol of a miracle. Was it just coincidence that I should walk into a toy store when I was away from home to find just what I needed when I didn't know it existed? Did the store clerk know Firey was waiting for me to find him?

On my way out the door the clerk asked me to take good care of my purchase, considering its rough treatment in the store. I assured him Firey would be loved and appreciated.

Firey has been through many dismemberments, as I myself have. Every time I look at him he reminds me that transitions don't have to be traumatic. The pieces (and the resultant growth) always come together to make me more of a survivor, ready for the next challenge!

If it is true that we teach what we need to learn, Firey has become for me a perfect symbol of the way my personal collection of "what ifs" can dismember me until I've lost my head and allowed an event to have power over me. Sitting on my couch, Firey sends his message to me each time I see him: "Don't lose your head!"

A Miracle Story

The Spider at My Door

A large yellow spider with a fat, round belly the size of a quarter has taken up residence in my front porch lamp at the edge of my door (see Fig. 18). What I call anchor lines form the foundation of the web. They are so strong they are virtually weatherproof, but the traditional circular spider web woven upon the anchor lines constantly needs repair.

My spider is a night spider that spends its days nestled under a projection of the lamp, surrounded securely by a woven tunnel attached to the web. At night Spider reworks

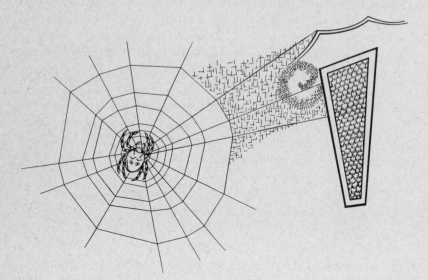

18: Spider at My Door
The spider is a symbol of the perseverance and patience necessary for pursuing goals.

the two-foot-diameter web or sits patiently at the center waiting for the dinner that will be attracted by the light to be deposited on its web.

At another time or place I might have struck the web down to discourage Spider. After all, the web is right over my front door. Some visitors have entered my home, commenting about Spider and web. I quickly thank them for telling me about it and ask them to let it alone. This spider I like; it means no harm.

I've learned much about life from my sporadic observations of this spider, which has become a metaphor for my life. In the time since David has died I have begun to believe in and depend upon networking for most of my survival. Networking is an exchange of information with my friends to support each other's activities, interests, and needs. For me, Spider's web is a symbol of networking. It is also an affirmation of interconnectedness. How symbolic and appropriate for this web to be strung over my front door! Like Spider, I would starve without my version of the web.

Just as the light attracts insects to the web and sustains Spider, word spread by friends about David's art attracts new friends and their resources into my home. They become sustenance for me, spiritually and financially. Since networking is a two-way avenue, then I, too, am some form of food in another's web!

The web is a symbol of faith in the abundant universe that deposits insects upon it for Spider's survival. Acting upon that principle, Spider repeatedly weaves and repairs the web. I do the same. I have often commented that I am fueled by faith in the network of connections. My web is my lifeline. And I am prompt to respond to opportunities that manifest within it. I weave the web and make connections with others I meet. Doing my part, acting responsibly with the references and ideas that come to me, I trust the universe to send those who will help me with my needs.

Even day after day of bad weather and destroyed web don't discourage Spider. Spiders can't afford to quit when they are met with the frustration of disintegrating webs. In spite of adversity, each night Spider is out on the web, reweaving, repairing, and renewing it. Spiders persevere, spinning web after web after web. And then they patiently wait and wait and wait, knowing that flying insects will land in the web.

The spider symbolizes my philosophy about the craftsmanship of life. No matter how discouraged I get with the outcome of my efforts, I must always keep the web in good condition. A well-connected web lands the tastiest morsels. Spiders who lose faith and stop weaving their webs aren't long for this world!

NOTES

1. The SilverHawk character names, SteelWill and StrongHold, are trademarks of Lorimar-Telepictures Corporation and are manufactured by Kenner Products in Cincinnati, Ohio.

2. Joseph Campbell, *The Power of Myth* (New York: Doubleday, 1988), Chapter V, "The Hero's Adventure."

3. "Joseph Campbell and the Power of Myth with Bill Moyers" is a film by Apostrophe S Productions, Incorporated, which appeared in 1988 on Public Television.

4. Labyrinth is a 1986 fantasy movie, directed by Jim Henson. Labyrinth and the names of its characters, like Firey, are trademarks of Henson Associates.

Epilogue
Using the Cards to Create Your Personal Ceremony

A ceremony is a story about a change in your attitude or your life that you act out with physical actions and symbols in front of a witness.

Use the cards bound with this book to help you design your own ceremony. The cards embody principles, aspects, or stages essential to the preparation of a meaningful ceremony and can serve as reminders of its various parts. You may want to use the supplemental blank cards to suit your needs.

Where to look. Information about creating a personal ceremony is in Chapter Three, Creating Your Personal Ceremony. If you want to involve a group of friends to celebrate your mutual growth, refer to Chapter Four, The Giveaway Celebration. "Putting on a Good Show" at the end of Chapter Three suggests ways to involve your senses to make the ceremony more effective. "Readings That May Be Included in Ceremonies" in Appendix A contains quotations that may be appropriate at different points in your celebration, or use other quotations that are meaningful to you.

Acting it out. In all of its stages, ceremony involves actions and symbols. The symbolic action that illustrates your story about the change is the most important action of all. Using actions with symbols in other parts of the ceremony is optional, but keep in mind that these symbolic actions contribute to the overall impact of the ceremony. This guide contains some suggestions for symbolic actions to accompany aspects of your ceremony.

Be creative. As you design your ceremony, you use your inner guidance, your intuitive sense, about what you need to do in it. Don't let the cards limit your creativity. They are meant only to stimulate it.

Stages of a Ceremony

A meaningful ceremony consists of two main parts, planning the ceremony and actually holding it. The Planning Cards ask you to think about the essential components of the ceremony: the location of the ceremony, the witness, the story, the symbol, and the action.

The Celebration Cards are designed for use in holding the ceremony. They help you decide what will actually take place to build upon the main concepts you've developed in the planning stage. Much of the celebration depends on the nature of the change and the elaborateness of the ceremony you plan. When you're dealing with a big, emotionally-charged change, the more friends you involve and the more elements you include, the more impact the ceremony will have upon your mind. Even the most simple ceremony, however, should include all of the planning cards (numbers 1–6) and have a beginning (numbers 7–9), a middle (number 10), and an end (number 14).

The Planning Cards

When you have decided you would like to create a ceremony to mark a change in your mind or your life, begin your planning by selecting the cards needed for advance preparation—card numbers 1 through 6.

Look at card number 1, "Name the Change." Think about the change you want to celebrate, what you want to affirm or release. Consider this card a symbol for the story about that change. If you wish, give your story a title. Decide the way you will describe the change to a friend. "Personal Storytelling" in Chapter Three contains different formats that may be helpful as you think about your story. Keep card number 1 in front of you so that you will remember to make your ceremony center around that particular change.

Now move to card number 2, "Symbols of Change." This card represents the physical symbol for your change. It asks you to find, create, or buy a symbol of release or affirmation about which your ceremony will center. For ideas in selecting a symbol of change, see the sections called "Symbols of Affirmation" and "Symbols of Release" in Chapter Two and "Symbols of Change" in Chapter Three. Or use something that approximates the concept as a substitute symbol, as described in Chapter Three.

Pick up card number 3, "Symbolic Action." How will you act upon the physical symbol of your change to make that change graphic and clear? Plan your action. Decide whether you want to involve your witness in some special way. For ideas on actions you may want to perform, see the section of Chapter Three, "Symbolic Action with Symbols," that explains how to act upon your symbol in order to reinforce the idea of change.

Now look at card number 4, "Personal Symbolism." This card helps you think about what you will wear and what personally significant symbols you will have with you that affirm your power. For ideas on what to wear and objects to use as part of the symbolic moment, refer to "Personal Symbols" in Chapter Two.

Card number 5, "Place & Time," is next. This card helps you decide where—in what special place—and when your ceremony will occur. Does the place and time have some special significance to you? "The Ceremony" in Chapter Three has a paragraph detailing this consideration. Think about the environment of the ceremony. What will you need to make the setting more dramatic? Review the suggestions in "Putting on a Good Show" in Chapter Three. Also consider your participants' comfort. Remember your camera or tape recorder if you'd like to document this special day.

Card number 6, "Witness," helps you determine who will be with you during the ceremony. Is this a private ceremony, or is it a group affair in which everyone describes changes they've experienced? Think about the way you want to involve your friends in the ceremony and what they will need to have with them if you want them to participate in a special way. When you have decided on witnesses or participants, send or phone your invitations. "Witnesses" in Chapter Three describes why it's important to include others to make the ceremony effective. Appendix B contains an invitation to a Giveaway ceremony, "An Invitation to the Celebration of Becoming."

The Celebration Cards

Use card numbers 7 through 14 to help you move through the celebration itself in a smooth, effective, enjoyable manner. These cards progress sequentially through the basic stages of a ceremony. After you have used them to design your ceremony, you may want to set them out in front of you as cue cards and to ensure that distractions will not keep you from covering all the important parts of the ceremony you have planned so carefully.

Begin with card number 7, "Opening." Tell your witness why this time and place are special. Sanctify the space and those of you in it with a blessing, and honor the energies of creation. You may want to burn incense or fragrant plant materials to symbolize purification and your prayers or use water as a symbolic cleanser. An opening meditation, prayer, song, or music helps to center the energies of the group. You may choose to use readings I've included in Appendix A: "Fires of Transformation," "The Morning Call," "Honoring the Directions," "Navajo Prayer," "The Charge of the Goddess." See Appendix B for a "Giveaway Ceremony Greeting."

Then look at card number 8, "Intent." This card tells you to begin your ceremony with a clear statement of its purpose. You—and others, if they are actively participating—should all state the reason they are present and the change they are celebrating. You may want to symbolize this intent with an accompanying action, such as having each person light a candle as he or she makes a brief statement of purpose, or by making a knot in a cord or ribbon ("Cord of Community," Chapter Four), or by mutually touching a special symbol.

Card number 9, "Personal Stories," reminds you to talk about the significance of what you're wearing, the symbols of power you have with you, and the special blessings you've recently experienced. Invite your friends to do the same. This type of storytelling helps strangers to become friends and to feel as if they're part of the "family." For ideas on wearing special clothing, refer to "Significance of Adornment and Personal Symbols" in Chapter Three. This is also a time to read favorite quotations, play music, or sing songs.

Now select card number 10, "The Change." This card is

the basic story-and-action card that refers to numbers 1–3 of the planning cards, which asked you to decide the way to talk about, symbolize, and act out your change. This is the time to say and show what you mean. Pay careful attention to what you're doing and what you're saying. As you speak of the change, you will perform your symbolic action of release, passage, or affirmation. The action, accompanied by your story, makes the change real for you and for the friends with you. This is also the time to tell any miracle stories that support the change you're making. Readings, songs, and music may be appropriate here, too.

Card number 11, "Affirmation/Commitment," comes next. This card reminds you to contract with yourself or your witness to carry out the change in the future. You symbolize this commitment, for example, by shaking hands, signing a written promise, or donning a new article of clothing. Other suggestions for making the commitment to a new life in the future may be found in two segments of Appendix B, "Action Contract" and "Personal Value Affirmations." Refer to "Personal Symbols of Affirmation" in Chapter Two if you want to remind yourself about your commitment on a regular basis. You may want to leave a prayer stick, described in Appendix B, to affirm your future good.

Winding Down

This part of the ceremony is a sort of a recapitulation. It is used to underline the more dramatic and meaningful actions that preceded it. For it you use card numbers 12–14.

Card number 12, "Food & Friendship," symbolizes thanksgiving for the grace of friendship, sustenance, and sharing of special moments. In this step of the ceremony you share a small amount of food and/or drink as you express gratitude for the gifts of friends, nourishment, and blessings that support you in your journey through life. You may want to symbolize this by feeding each other a bit of food, by drinking from the same cup, or by making a toast. Describe why the food or drink is significant to you. Readings, songs, and music may be appropriate here, too. For more suggestions, see "Apple of Delight" and "Saying Grace at Meals" in Appendix B.

Card number 13, "Renewal," asks you to think of ways to affirm and symbolize your new beginning. Saying the Beautyway Prayer and having your witness encircle you with cornmeal are ways to symbolically affirm the way you have changed and your anticipation of the future. This prayer and other suggestions are in Chapter Three, "The Ceremony." Readings, songs, and music can be used to affirm your symbolic renewal. Suggested readings in Appendix A are: "Resistance to Change," "Modified Sufi Blessing," "The Warrior Shaman," and "The Joy of Death."

Card number 14, "Closing," reminds you to thank the energies of creation you honored as you began the ceremony for their participation and guidance. Thank your friends for their support and love at this special time. Share final comments about the ceremony. You may want to use readings, songs, and music as part of your closing. Then make a formal statement that the ceremony is finished. Symbolize this completion by extinguishing candles lit as you began the ceremony, or by cutting the knotted cord. A suggested reading, "Prayer from Amonophis I," is in Appendix A. A final card bears the blessing:

> Love is the source,
> Joy is the power,
> Life is the celebration!

Appendix A
Readings That May Be Included in Ceremonies

Fires of Transformation

(Quoted from David)

(This passage relates to burning incense, cedar and sage, or other fragrant plant materials. The four elements and cardinal directions are represented when plant materials are burned in an abalone shell: plants = earth, the north; smoke = air, the east; the burning of the plant material = fire, south; the shell = water, west.)

It is the custom with many Native Americans to use the symbol of fire as transformation. It is only through the flame of our lives, the trials, the burning away, that we become a living prayer. To run from the challenges we face in our personal growth and in our lives is to ignore the greatest gift that the Creator has given us—the gift of our own passions, our own sufferings, and our resultant transformation.

The Morning Call

(Quoted from David)

Although I'm half-Navajo, I was raised among the Pueblo Indians as much as I was in my own tribe. The Pueblo Indians began each day with the Morning Call. We looked at a day as not "just another day" but as a specific commitment to life, to the now. The appointed leader for that day would climb to the highest rooftop in the pueblo and call the prayer in the native language. This is a translation:

"I must always strive to remember I am a privileged guest in this sacred place. I am here both to enjoy and edify its beauty. Let me reach out and touch others who may be blinded to the gifts of creation, reminding them that our hosts, Mother Earth and Father Sky, wish only to share love. Wonderment and awe they also share. These are the gifts they offer. In this house, their house, let me learn to not only tend and nurture the wondrous environment but also offer my fellow guests a share of my visions, hopes, and aspirations that they may not leave this place in shame."

Resistance to Change

(Quoted from David)

Being in love is to give up the past for the glory of the now. To be in love is to share, to flow into the universe and each other, to dance the dance of life, and to know the Creator because you are one with that spirit. As long as we experience life as resistance to change and transformation, we don't stand a "ghost of a chance."

Dance of the Medicine Man

(David's recollection)

Gabriel sat quietly by the fire, shoulders hunched. Deep furrows etched by the experience of many years appeared as mysterious lines of some ancient script imprinted on the fragile fabric of his face.

In the silence I could almost hear his thoughts forming as he struggled to find the right words to say. For this was to be our final moment of sharing.

"David," he said. "David, never forget how to dance. Dance the dance of the medicine man. Call upon the spirit of our ancestors and listen to the music of their wisdom, the drumming of their hearts, and the quiet chanting of their voices. Then dance. Dance to the music of their spirit as it mixes with the sound of your dreams. Dance, David! Dance and you will never be alone. I will be with you, dancing in your footsteps, singing with your voice, healing through your hands, and loving through your heart."

His gnarled hand brushed mine, and then he was led away to the sanctuary of his kiva, the sacred meeting place of our clan. That night Gabriel Reano died, only to be reborn in the hearts of those he loved.

Honoring the Directions

Let us bless and consecrate the ground and the four directions, the above and the below, honoring the energies of the earth and the sky, asking them to share their wisdom with us. This is our sacred space. The circle is symbolic of the universe, of life never-ending.

East: symbolic of enlightenment, morning, inspiration; element of air; season of spring.

South: symbolic of action in the world; midday; summer; element of fire; season of summer.

West: symbolic of the element of water; those things that hold water or come from water—shells, bowls; evening; season of autumn.

North: symbolic of powers of the night, dreams; pause between the harvest and planting; wisdom of the ancestors (those who have lived before us); element of earth; season of winter.

The above and the below, Father Sky and Mother Earth, are the fifth and sixth directions.

The seventh direction is inside each of us, symbolic of the personal path we choose to follow in life.

Navajo Prayer

(From David)

Let us pause for a moment and reflect upon the beauty that is Mother Earth and Father Sky, and ask their blessing for those of us gathered together and for those present in our hearts.

> Oh our Mother, the earth,
> Oh our Father, the sky,
> Your children are we.
> We bring you a gift of love,
> that you may weave us a garment of
> brightness.
> May the warp be the white light of morning,
> May the weft be the red light of evening,
> May the fringes be the falling rain,
> May the border be the standing rainbow.

Thus weave for us a garment of brightness,
That we may walk fittingly where birds sing,
that we may walk fittingly where grass is green.
Oh our Mother, the earth,
Oh our Father, the sky,
Bless all who are gathered here today,
And bless all who dwell upon this land.

Modified Sufi Blessing

May the blessings of love rest upon you.
May love's peace abide with you.
May love's presence illuminate your heart,
now and forever more.

Prayer from Amonophis I

(Channeled through David)

Build me a temple, not of stone but of kindly
words.
Surround it with soldiers armed not with spears but
with song.
At the capstone of my pyramid place not gold but
pure shining light.
Let my war cry be laughter.
Let there be no mourning in my kingdom.
For my soldiers and my subjects will not die by the
sword
But shall be lifted up on clouds of love,
Accompanied by the winds of peace.
Soft rains shall fall upon my valleys.

And even the peaks of my mighty mountains shall
Burst forth with the scent of flowers sweeter than
the lotus
And more pungent than the breath of God.

The Charge of the Goddess

(This anonymous pagan invocation appears in print in varying forms.)

I who am the beauty of the green earth and the white
  moon upon the mysteries of the waters,
I call upon you to arise and come unto me.
For I am the soul of nature that gives life to the universe.
From me all things proceed, and unto me they must
  return.
Let my worship be in the heart that rejoices.
For behold, all acts of love and pleasure are my rituals.
Let there be beauty and strength, power and compassion,
  honor and humility, mirth and reverence within you.
And you who seek to know me, know that the seeking
  and yearning will avail you not unless you know the
  mystery.
For if that which you seek you find not in yourself,
  you will never find it without.
For behold, I have been with you from the beginning,
  and I am that which is attained at the end of desire.

The Warrior-Shaman

(This was David's closing address to the participants of a shamanic workshop.)

I want to discuss the concept of the warrior-shaman. This doesn't mean a warrior in the traditional sense of the shaman picking up a spear and fighting the evil forces. True warriors take the arrows into themselves. They become wounded through these wounds. In healing themselves the shamans find a strength, then, to reach out and to heal others.

They experience these wounds as gifts, as opportunities. Through whatever ordeals they experience, whether it is getting rid of everything they have, or manifesting an illness in their lives, or a great sadness or confusion, it is to be able to take that wound and to wear it proudly. It is to bear the scars of life, not as a shield but as a big, open place for everything to come into them.

To be truly brave is to lay down all of the weapons and to stand naked in the midst of the foe. It is to hear the foe crying and to change those tears to laughter. The shamans know those wounds are not theirs, but the world's. Those pains are not theirs, but Mother Earth's. Those tears are nothing but the purifying rain.

Each of you as warrior-shamans has suffered many tiny wounds, none of them big enough to make you feel as if you're strong. If you stand back from your body and look at it, you may think that you've lived a pretty nice life, yet there are many tiny wounds. You almost look like a screen that you can see through. Those wounds have opened you up; you can use them as gifts. You can gift the world as shaman because you're a wounded warrior.

A wounded healer and a wounded warrior are one. We can

embrace because we've been pushed away. We can heal because we've been torn apart. We can touch people's minds because we have lost our own. We can speak wisdom because our tongues have been cut off and our voices have been denied. We can run like the wind because our legs have been broken.

The shaman as a warrior is you and your ability to not just heal from what you have experienced but also to know that your experience is *every* person's experience. This puts you in touch with every man, every woman, every wounded animal, every "bent cloud." Your shaking, your fevers, and your fears put you in touch with the earth. You don't have to touch the earth to know that it is shaking, because it is shaking through you. You know that it is time to heal. All of us together, as brothers and sisters, are relatives.

Now it is time to regain the power, to take more arrows into our hearts so that we are stronger, to let the demons trample us so that we can stand straighter, to let the freezing winds pierce our hearts so that we can love more, so that we can constantly purify ourselves by being the true warrior.

The warrior-shaman is not the one who throws the spear but the one who rises above his own dead body and says, "I have died, too! Now let's dance! We're free! The spirit is ours because we have died. Now, we are resurrected from the ashes. Come dance with me, sisters, brothers, relatives! I can never be alone because I have died. My ashes have blown to the wind. My blood has run into the earth. My bones have whitened and flowed into the clouds. I can never be alone again."

The symbol of the shaman is the dying, the going back into the underworld to experience our own wounds, to see our own death, to experience it, to arise as a warrior whose only weapon is love. The wounds we have suffered through life's experiences have all killed us. Each time we take in a breath and hold it, we die. Each time we breathe out, our breath touches the face of all humankind, all animals, all of our ancestors, all of our relatives. This is the warrior-shamans' vision. They know that they have died, and because of that, they are one with everything.

We're lucky as shamans. We're lucky to be warriors. We know we have died. We have been wounded, and we're here to heal.

Each and every one of you is a strong and powerful warrior. Every one of you deserves your feather, which is a symbol of your spirit reaching out because you have died.

In the warrior societies of the native tribes, you don't get your spirit feather until you have died, until you have been wounded, until you have been hurt. That doesn't mean "until you've done battle in the field." It may have been that you have lain in your bed and trembled and cried, or that you've been torn apart by the "word-arrows" of someone else.

When you're very young, you're given your first feather because in being born you have died. You've left the safe womb, the home, to come out into the world of spirits that have manifested flesh, and you have died. One of my friends has told me that when you die, you are more alive than you think you are when you're alive.

The warrior-shaman knows the feather is a symbol of the breath that goes out. The sage that is burnt is a symbol of the spirit going out and touching everything.

We have the privilege of serving others, of reaching out to them. We can share with others that they have died and are reborn. Even Christ said that you're not alive until you're born again. The shaman is a warrior who has experienced that kind of death, before physically dying.

Every one here is a tall, proud warrior. Your scars, your death, is our life. Thank you for dying, for sharing, for accepting the privilege to serve others as a shaman.

They say that when you acknowledge you are a shaman, all the spirits in the underworld sing with joy, and all the spirits in the upper world echo that joy. That joy manifests every time you touch someone in healing. Let it be done in beauty. It is our way. It is the Beauty Way.

Unless we get too serious—you can tell people that you're born again. You're a born-again shaman!

Divisiveness Within Human Society

(Channeled through David)

All the information that has been gathered seems to indicate that when myth or creative response becomes frozen and is related directly to time, space, [and] culture, it immediately becomes divisive by nature. [It is] the failure to recognize that all creative response is pure creative energy and must not be limited [that] leads to a divisive structure. A pattern is set that separates it from another pattern. The ocean of consciousness is no longer fed by the streams and rivers of the universal experience and becomes stagnant.

One must un-dam the streams. One must allow for the natural flow of the creative spirit, or one limits not only one's experiences but the experiences of others, condemning them to one form of stagnation or another. In the slime of the stagnated stream and the stagnated ocean one finds a return to the primal forms. The well springs dry up, and the sea becomes a barren land, and the land is no longer fed. An entity dies, unrefreshed, unfed, [and] un-nourished.

The solution lies within the ability of consciousness to force new pathways, to open up new tributaries, to feed the ocean of consciousness freely. For consciousness itself is stagnating. We speak of the earth consciousness, the consciousness of humankind, becoming parched, barren of symbols, barren of images, denied the refreshment of new rains.

Perhaps this is the anxiety that is being felt by some [people]—the knowledge that the wellspring is drying while others try to hold the last drop of water of consciousness to them, to protect it, to call it their own. By doing so they condemn themselves and others to the final drought. Perhaps the great droughts that are predicted by your prophets, by your seers, by your shamans, are not droughts that will destroy the land, but droughts that are already destroying the spirit, denying the nourishment that is primary to universal growth.

The Joy of Death

(Channeled through David)

The gift of accepting the spirit within ourselves allows us to die to this moment and move on to the next moment. This is the joy of death. Let us never cling to life so tightly that we deny death. Death is what allows us to release the old and accept the new. Death allows us the next moment. It allows us to be born again into the present. Now is death. It is the still moment of death within everyone that renews. Death and transition are life and creation itself. Let us celebrate death by accepting our continual rebirth and renewal. Life is becoming, one moment to the next. Death is a symbol of becoming.

Appendix B
Ceremonies, Stories, Symbols, and Actions

An Invitation to the Celebration of Becoming

(A Giveaway Ceremony Invitation)

I invite you to join me in a Celebration of Becoming. It is a time of harvesting the gifts of growth we have experienced in the past year, a time of looking back and moving on. Please bring a dish to contribute to the potluck for the physical nourishing of our bodies after we have celebrated the perfection of our spirits.

For me, this gathering is an affirmation of the community spirit that binds us together in the sense of sisterhood and/or brotherhood. I believe that a sense of community is the best "insurance policy" we can have. Together, we have the resources to address our needs in the continual celebration of "becoming" that is life itself.

First, there will be a sharing of stories about the gifts we have gained from the experiences of the year; then we will release what has been transformed. How are we different from last year? Here are some thoughts to direct your reflection: "These gifts I have gathered. These beliefs I have transformed. This I have gained. This I release. This is my story. This is my prayer (for myself, for the planet). This is my hope. This I claim for myself."

Then there will be a time to recognize those things that have passed out of our lives. What symbol will you bring to the Giveaway that represents a change in your life or your thinking? What object best relates to that change? These symbols of the past are a letting go to make room for something new as we celebrate and affirm our continual blossoming, transition, and transformation.

At the close of the celebration all participants will be individually blessed with cornmeal as they each read the Beautyway Prayer. This is a symbolic affirmation of our renewal and rebirth.

These are the "bones" of the ritual. It is up to each of us to add "flesh" to these bones through the energy of our creativity to make it a genuine celebration. Please bring any readings that are meaningful to you. Suggestions for music and movement are welcome. A cassette player will be available.

I look forward to your unique way of sharing and celebrating within the circle of friendship and community.

Giveaway Ceremony Greeting

This is the council of wisdom that is abundant in resources. We draw upon the wisdom that is beyond our minds through our bodies, manifesting and integrating it into ourselves. Then we take that power as a spider does to spin the web of creation, the stories of our lives.

"The story you tell yourself is the life you bring forth. As you tell it, it begins to happen. Choose wisely your story, the image you bring forth from your mind. A people without a dream perish because they have no future."[1]

We are as gods and goddesses manifesting our dreams into reality. At each moment we stand between the manifest and the unmanifest. We are being asked to acknowledge our power to create ourselves and our world perfectly. We can do it. Each of us is powerful.

We have come together to share the richness in our hearts, the lessons and growth that we have harvested in this year. We offer words from our hearts. We are witnesses to each other's beauty and strength of spirit.

We have come to celebrate the community that we form. This is the safe harbor and the resource of love and support that helps us weather the storms we experience in our lives. It is safe here to share with each other because we come in the spirit of unconditional love and acceptance. We recognize the sacred web of our interconnectedness, dancing between the unity and the illusion of our separation. Each of us is a note in the symphony of life; each of us is a thread in the tapestry of becoming.

Let this gathering affirm the meaning and beauty of life. Let us commit to the healing of this planet however we may choose, knowing that the opportunities for healing on all levels are always present for us to act upon. Let us live our lives with integrity. Let each of us walk in beauty.

Personal Growth Stories of Affirmation

Please share with us your story about the gifts you have experienced through the events in your life. What have you gained? What truths have you transformed? What is your story?

The Giveaway—Stories of Release

What has passed out of your life? What do you release? How do you choose to symbolize your transition? Telling the story and releasing your symbol is an affirmation of your personal power and your continual blossoming transition and transformation.

Taking Affirmative Action

Personal Value Affirmations

As you decide upon steps to manifest the desired change you stated in your ceremony, think about the personal value it reflects. Why is it important for you to accomplish your stated goal? Write an affirmation to support this underlying value. If, for instance, your goal is to spend more quality time with your family, the underlying value affirmation may be, "I love my family."

Losing track of the personal value that originally motivated the goal can transform it into just another task or obligation. When that feeling arises, it may be time to refocus upon the original value to determine whether it is still valid for you. Value affirmations help to focus upon the motivating value of the goal and decrease the resistance to change. Whatever the goal, working toward its fulfillment, or actually accomplishing it, creates a sense of self-esteem and personal fulfillment because it reflects something important to you.

Action Contract

After making a commitment to create a change in your life, to move in another less familiar direction or act another way to reflect your belief, it is important to take action on that commitment. An action contract is a way to help you "walk your talk." Words are easy, but actions are the proof of the commitment to change. To become reality, dreams need action.

An action contract or "behavioral contract"[2] begins by naming an activity that supports your new direction. Or it might be a project you've been putting off because of outside pressures.

Tell a loving, supportive friend you will accomplish the project of your choice by a specific date. Decide how you will reward yourself to celebrate your success when you complete it. Your friend may also name a project, a completion date, and a reward for fulfillment.

Mutually creating expectations in each other's mind can provide the support that's been missing to spur both of you to action. For projects that have been continually delayed, action contracts are a creative solution to procrastination!

As an additional incentive, you might select a valued possession and give it to your friend to return to you at the completion of the project. You may even agree to forfeit the object if you don't finish your project by the stated date. This is your action contract; you know what completing the project means to you and how high you should set the stakes to motivate yourself to act.

Affirmation Signal

Create an affirmation, or memorize something that lifts and affirms your spirit. Each time you're waiting at a traffic light, use the red light to signal your mind to focus upon that thought or to visualize your goal.

This is a great technique for changing unproductive habits. When I recognized that I needed to change my habit of succumbing to panic and breathing shallowly, I used the signal to remind me to breathe more deeply while I affirmed feeling calm and peaceful.

A Celebration of Life Monument Park

Once when I was wandering through a cemetery full of professional and do-it-yourself monuments, I delighted in the many creative expressions of memorializing a person and mused about the varieties of religious symbols used in the monument designs. Because many of my friends have grown past the limitations of traditional religions, I wondered what symbols could be used for their monuments if they were to be buried in a cemetery. Although most of my friends want to be cremated, I amused myself wondering what designs would more accurately reflect their beliefs. A rush of symbols filled my mind: dolphins, rainbows, butterflies, sun, moon, stars, crystals, shells, feathers, hearts, figures from fantasy and myth, gods, and goddesses.

I read the usual sayings on the markers: "Gone, but not Forgotten," "Rest in Peace," and "Safe in the Arms of Jesus." These sayings affirm the usual sense of separation of the dead from the living. I smiled with delight as I noticed one monument depicting an eagle with "Free as a Bird" carved in the stone.

The memory of a transcript I'd typed came to mind. Nihir, an unseen Egyptian entity, was speaking to a workshop David was leading: "The greatest mystery I ever pondered about as Nihir was the question of why we were pursuing an elusive future instead of celebrating the wondrous gifts that were present. Why were we continually building monuments for others instead of building monuments to ourselves?...Why are you not experiencing the monument that you are and the fullness, richness, completeness of your own nature?"

How would I symbolize myself today to celebrate the monument that I am? What symbols and words would I use to reflect my philosophy and attitude about my life experience? I thought of the happy Buddha with his upraised arms. Inscribed on his robust belly was my affirmation, "Love is the source, joy is the power, life is the celebration!" My mind was off racing, oblivious to practical limitations. I watched my monument grow in my mind's eye as I added pinwheels and other wind toys. Glorious and exotic flowers sprang up around the marker. Then with a giggle I designed a phoenix in neon light and added multicolored blinking lights to symbolize spirit sparkle. It wasn't long before I was laughing out loud at the shape-shifting image in my mind.

By affirming the experience of life, a Celebration of Life Monument Park would contrast with the cemetery monuments to those who had died. I mused that it might look like a sculpture garden to inspire and uplift others' spirits. Some monuments might be sophisticated and subdued; others might look colorful and primitive. Each unique monument would symbolize an individual expression of the creative spirit that unites us all. Perhaps this park would encourage others to try their hands at symbolizing themselves and affirming their lives.

I decided to invite my friends to a potluck to explore their ideas, and I sent out the following invitation:

Dear very creative person and most illustrious of spirit sparkle!

You are cordially invited to an afternoon of creative imagination and fantasy. The subject of exploration is a Celebration of Life Monument Park. Cemeteries emphasize monuments to those who have passed on; I've decided we need to create a variation on the theme by celebrating life.

Let's not wait for our survivors to create monuments to us after we're gone. Let's build a monument to ourselves now! If you want the job done right, you've got to do it yourself! Besides, you know yourself better than anyone else does!

147

Don't take me literally unless you want to. This is something we build in our minds and then describe as best we can. Please bring with you a "monument"al idea expressed in words, images, symbols, favorite quotations, whatever. This is a "no-holds-barred" brazen exploration of the way you would symbolize or create a monument to yourself and your experience of life. What wisdom have you gathered in all these years of character-building that might be useful to others who would visit this inspirational park? What are the most meaningful elements of yourself (and life) to you?

Imagine a beautiful grassy park sprinkled liberally with trees, fantastic flowers, birds, and so on. A sense of beauty, peace, and joy permeates this magical place. Perhaps there's a fountain sculpture at the center of this park: what does it look like? Radiating from the center of the park are paths in a spider-web design to symbolize the interconnectedness of our lives.

Other people are arriving and finding a place to create on the spot, instantly, a monument to themselves that expresses their current experience of life. Everyone present, including you, is endowed with a magical ability to manifest his or her idea into form. There are no limitations; everything is possible. Your monument can be as intricate or as simple, as solemn or as playful as you'd like to make it. Maybe this monument will inspire a viewer to think about life in another way.

Bring your idea, no matter what shape it takes. Perhaps it will grow and change even as you describe it to those who attend this gathering. I'm looking forward to exploring the evolution of this celebration park as we combine our ideas and meander mentally through a thought-form that is collectively greater than we could imagine alone.

Joy to My World: A Celebration of Spirit Renewal

Hold a festival of candlelight to affirm the personal growth that has been "en-lightening" for you, something that has given more light and spark to your spirit. Use this occasion to pay attention to the past events that have had positive effects on your life. The ending of the calendar year (or the end of a phase of your life, or your birthday) is a great time to reflect on this subject before entering the New Year (or the next period of life). By focusing on moments when things have gone well, we can find more spiritual strength to confidently face the uncertainties of the future. Although this ceremony can be done alone, being in the presence of other friends who value their growth multiplies the love and joy as the stories are shared around the circle.

You may decide to use candles to mark the past, the present, and the future; or they may relate to specific events or different aspects of your life (relationships, family, health, finances, business, and spiritual growth). Light a candle each time you speak about a different subject. Play some uplifting music. Burn your favorite incense.

Use these questions to guide your reflections: What spirit survival tools have you gathered that will help you to more easily cope with change in your life? Think of ways you have creatively resolved this year's (phase's) challenges. Anything that added to your sense of happiness and harmony can be recognized. How did you love and nurture yourself? What desires have you had in the past that are now manifest as your present experience? What things in your life are you grateful for now? What miracles have happened to you? Were you a miracle in another's life?

Write down on paper those things that weighed upon your spirit, the painful events or difficult times. Burning them symbolically affirms the release of those things in the year that burdened and dispirited you. Remember, they've been good teachers because you've learned something positive from them. They may even be disguised blessings. Release the pain. Affirm the gain. Take a moment to meditate upon the year with some peaceful music in the background as you allow the fire to transform and release the pain from your life.

After celebrating the present state of your "en-lightened" spirit by affirming the gain and releasing the pain, name your desired future experience. Play music that creates a sense of strength and triumph.

Feel the joy in yourself and your life. Feel how powerful and successful you are with your ability to attract your desires. Create an image in your mind of the beauty and love you have now, which will continue into your future. See it growing ever greater as your heart glows brighter and brighter. Picture yourself being, doing, and having your desires as though they were an accomplished fact. Feel the joy of living your ideal life right now in your mind. Release the visual prayer to the abundant universe with "This or something better now manifests for me in totally satisfying and harmonious ways for the highest good of all concerned."³ Celebrate that vision by lighting a special candle.

After visualizing your desired reality you may be more clear about the experiences you'd like to have to help you explore more of your creative potential. Write down those dreams and decide what you'd most like to achieve in this next period of time.

Celebrate your renewed spirit with your favorite food. Give your blessing and your prayers to the source of the food, and surround the planet with your healing love. You might want to close your ceremony with "The Morning Call" (see Appendix A).

Apple of Delight

Share an apple with a friend. Before eating it, invest it with good thoughts. As you hold the apple, affirm the beauty and harmony within your world, your present source of spirit sparkle. Name your desires for the future—those things that will help your spirit to glow even brighter than it is glowing today. Generate a sense of joy to empower yourself and energize your affirmations. Joy is a powerful emotion. Acting as witness for each other, pass the apple back and forth between you as the ideas come to mind. Visualize the apple containing the good energy each time you speak and hold it.

When you have finished nourishing your spirits, eat the apple as an act of communion. Direct your attention while you're eating to energize your thoughts, and bless the apple for nourishing your bodies.

Any piece of fruit or other food will work. What matters are the ideas, the intention, and the action. The more people who participate, the greater the energy!

Ceremony and Hospitals

Hospitalization can be a desensitizing and dehumanizing experience. In the impersonal environment of a hospital, a ceremony can be therapeutic when it directs your attitude about the experience in a positive, self- and life-affirming way. This is no time to feel like a powerless victim. Tailor the following exercise to your specific needs, focusing upon your mental ability to participate in your healing.

If you have elected to have surgery, a ceremony can help you establish a positive attitude about the surgeon and the surgery.

Story. Create a story to affirm your positive attitude about the surgery. Include the way you are feeling about it, mentally, emotionally, and physically. Describe why you need it, your confidence in the surgeon's skill, the way it will improve your condition, the way you visualize your recovery, the way the surgery will affect your future. Your counsel with the surgeon and other professionals is part of your wisdom story.

Symbols. Consult your inner healer to decide upon the symbols that will be most meaningful to use. You may choose to use metaphors instead of detailing the anatomical change. How will you symbolize what you are releasing and affirming? What symbolizes your personal power and spiritual strength to help you endure what your hospital stay entails? Will you have a symbol that affirms your power to heal?

Witnesses. Who will witness your words and actions? If you have a comfortable relationship with the surgeon, it would be desirable to include him or her in a short ceremony. If you know others who will be assisting you while you're hospitalized, you may want to include them in parts of a ceremony. Use it to link yourself to those friends and professionals who are supporting you.

Ceremony. With focused intent and awareness, and in the presence of a supportive witness or witnesses (the more, the merrier), illustrate your story by acting upon your symbols in some meaningful way. Know that you are symbolically communicating with the subconscious part of your mind and that it accepts what you sincerely believe to be true as *the truth*. You are enlisting the aid of this powerful ally in helping you to actualize what you are affirming. Don't forget to have fun in the process; it's your show!

Healing with Symbols

Acting regularly upon a physical object to symbolize the process of gradual healing helps objectify the desired result and state it clearly to the mind. Using full focused intent and verbally stating the significance of the symbols and the actions performed can amplify the mental imagery and affirmations that are part of a healing program.

For those who have difficulty clearly visualizing the desired results in their bodies, working on the physical level with tangible symbols to affirm the process of healing may lead to results similar to those achieved with mental visualization. If what is imagined in the mind affects the body, then physical imagery may also affect healing.

Allow your inner healer to intuitively direct the selection of the most appropriate symbol and action. Concentrate upon the meaning of the action on the symbol to affirm that the same thing is happening within the body. Like mental affirmations, the physical affirmation should be performed on a regular basis. Visualize the healing as accomplished each time you perform your symbolic action, although the actual process will occur over time. Check periodically with your inner guidance about the action and symbols. It may be necessary to change them to more appropriately meet your healing needs.

Applying water to a dry sponge (or raisins) could symbolize vitalizing energy to something that has shriveled and lost its function. Pouring hot water over sugar or salt could affirm a dissolving process. Squeezing water out of a sponge could affirm the healing of something that is swollen or inflamed.

A Morning Ritual: Starting the Day with a Spark in the Heart!

For the purpose of this ritual, record onto a cassette three musical pieces that correspond to the themes below, and then use the music to guide your thoughts when you begin the day.

Love is the source. Play music to evoke a feeling of peace and images of harmony to center yourself. Align with the Divine, the source of inspiration and creativity that comes to you during the day.

Joy is the power. Play music that evokes a sense of joy or lightens your heart. Joy is the power and energy to creatively respond to life.

Life is the celebration! Play music that inspires physical movement, such as music with drumming, or a parade march. As you move your body with the music, make symbolic gestures that graphically affirm your sense of centeredness and your connection with your world. Evoke a sense of aliveness and spiritual wonderment that will help you celebrate the day.

Prayer Stick

Symbolize your desires for the future with a created object made from organic material so that it will disintegrate naturally. Travel to some place in nature that is meaningful to you and leave the object there as a visible prayer of thanksgiving and affirmation for your future good. Take along a friend to witness your words and actions, or tell someone about it later. Celebrate with a picnic. This can be a way to mark significant anniversaries, honoring the past, celebrating the present, and affirming the future.

Prayer Flag

The Tibetans have a tradition of using prayer flags and prayer wheels. A prayer is written on paper and inserted into the cylinder of the prayer wheel. As the person rotates it, the prayer is believed to be released into the elements to find its destination. A breeze blowing past a prayer flag is believed to take the prayer inscribed on the fabric with it to the spirit realm. For the same purpose, the American Indians use a feather tied to a bush or tree. It symbolizes a prayer directed to the gods when the wind blows through it.

In our culture we have cylindrical wind socks, which we can decorate with our hopes, prayers, dreams, goals. I gave a wind sock to friends who were planning to move away. The cylinder was made of strips of rainbow-colored fabric; more colored strips hung from the bottom to flutter in the breeze. To the wind sock, I attached heart- and star-shaped brads used to decorate clothing to represent my wishes for love and luck in their new home. Colored stickers of flowers and birds added more color and good thoughts.

My friends were waiting for some things to happen before they could complete their move. I suggested that they write out their goals on paper and attach them to the flag as a primitive way to make their desires known to the gods. Because the subconscious mind relates more strongly to images than to words, I encouraged them to supplement their written words with photos from magazines and drawn designs of themselves enjoying their desired reality.

Some paper wishes disappeared with the wind. The ink faded on others. Some remained to blow in the breeze.

Some problems my friends faced grew worse and then were resolved in remarkable and unexpected ways. I encouraged them to acknowledge these "miracles" by affixing thank-you notes to the flag. They chose the green strip and called it their winning streak. Reviewing the thank-you notes helped them to recognize that things worked out in different ways and on a different time schedule than they expected. When they felt discouraged they were able to feel more optimistic about their situation because they had a visible record of the previous miracles on the flag to remind them about what had gone right in their recent past.

This is another way to nourish the mind with the health food of optimism to replace the junk food of anxiety and worry about uncertain outcomes. Cultivating an awareness of the way things ultimately work out for the best strengthens our relationship with and faith in a higher power, divinity, or God. An invisible source of support, guidance, and love is omnipresent for each of us. When you get what you've asked for, don't forget to say thanks!

Charitable Giveaways

Is there something you're symbolically releasing when you donate your clothes or personal items to a charitable organization? As you place the item in the collection box, think about what you are releasing and what you are affirming with that action. Make it significant to your mind.

A woman donated a hat that was too small for her head. She affirmed that she was releasing ideas that limited her intellectual and spiritual growth. A friend pinned a note on her deceased mother's coat before she donated it, wishing the new owner warmth and love, and signed it with her mother's name.

Cultivating Spirit Sparkle

Suggestions

Photograph your progress. Honor and document your spiritual growth and personal transformation. Take photos to record the significant events in life to reflect your progress and success. Have someone photograph you when you are doing something meaningful in your professional or personal life.

Make the time to affix these photos onto the pages of a special album. This is yourself on the path of becoming and blossoming. Reviewing these photographs brings back memories and shows you how fast your life is changing. Affirm your active participation and creative response to your growth from the circumstances in your life.

Photograph your friends and those people who are important to you. This is your community. Photograph the symbols you give away and those on your shrine of strength.

Document the actual experience of something you had visualized and affirmed earlier. You're more powerful than you think you are!

I had a friend photograph me standing in a museum exhibition room hung with David's paintings. What I had visualized and affirmed in my mind had become reality. Now I am more confident that museum shows are possible, when it wasn't long ago that I thought they would never happen!

When I gave my first presentation on ceremonies I photographed the group and was photographed during the talk. This was a big change in my life, since I instead of David was doing the talking.

Nurture yourself. If your habit has been to address others' needs before your own, begin to think of ways to treat yourself to something special. Cultivate an inner friend to help you address your needs and desires. Train yourself to notice the things in your life that are going well. Don't expect someone else to read your mind or to make you happy; dare to do things for yourself once in a while instead of to please others or fulfill their expectations.

Give yourself gifts, because you deserve to elevate your spirit. Happiness is an inside job. Remember whom you will never be without—yourself!

Fill your life with recorded music that helps you to feel happy. Find books that inspire you to grow spiritually and personally. Indulge yourself with a book that's just plain fun. Learn to love and delight in yourself and the special little pleasures of life. Notice the sunset, the moon, stars, flowers, trees, birds. Enjoy the taste of special foods. Have a good time with yourself. You will have more vitality to share with others.

Symbols, celebration, and personal growth journal. Create a journal to document your changing beliefs, the symbols and ceremonies you create, the miracles that have happened, healing stories you've told to others. Collect quotations that inspire you. Include whatever affirms yourself or your beliefs and that helps you celebrate the changes in your life. When you feel discouraged, refer to this book as an antidote to despair.

Time capsule cassettes. If your life is too demanding to allow you to write in a journal, you might use a tape recorder to capture your accomplishments as they happen, prefacing your comments with the date of each recording. Anything that has gone well or caused you to feel joy is fair game, including the simple things in life that give you pleasure. If you have a special supportive friend, you may choose to record your words as you talk on the phone or in person. At the end of the year the cassette can become a "time capsule" to help you remember special moments that might otherwise escape your recall. As time goes by and the tapes mount up, you will have a way to recall the years that have passed so rapidly.

If you have children, you might encourage them to record their own tape of accomplishments and good news during the year, to help them build self-esteem. Make duplicates of the tape to share with special family members and friends as holiday gifts, to allow others to applaud the children's success and growth.

Gifts with stories. Write down special stories you've created to heal and affirm others. How have you used your creativity to symbolize healing with a gift? Make up a story to go with the chicken soup you give to a sick friend. Don't wait until the holidays to appreciate your business associates and other professionals who assist you. Give them some token of appreciation (I use cookies) when they least expect it, and wrap it up with a story. Share those stories with your friends to help them begin to develop this special talent for helping others to feel good about themselves.

Saying grace at meals. Your mindful awareness can direct the spiritual essence, the *manna*, of food to manifest in the lives of those who are starving.

David believed that prayers said by the Sisters of Charity for him and others lost, missing, or presumed dead during World War II helped him survive his coma as he lay in a prison camp infirmary. The Sisters set a plate at each meal to symbolize those whom they prayed for. The act of saying grace connected those who ate the food with those who would be nourished on an unconscious level by the spiritual essence of the food.

During the time the media were reporting starvation in Ethiopia, David shared this idea in a lecture, suggesting that it was another way we could "send aid" to all who were suffering. This is his suggestion for grace at mealtime:

"Let us be constantly mindful of our need to honor the spirit of abundance that is shared with us by the Creator and of our need to share that abundance with those whose awareness of that spirit has been blinded through physical want and suffering. Let us affirm the richness and fullness provided by the Creator through all that is shared, in love, with others."

Symbols

Mystery and miracles. Record or symbolize the miraculous events in your recent and distant past. Think of metaphors describing the event, metaphors that may lead to a visual image or symbol. Did your ship come in? Were you able to fit the pieces together of something that had puzzled you? What's happened just when you needed it the most and expected it the least? These strange coincidences you've experienced can help you celebrate the mystery and wisdom of the unseen guidance operating within your life.

Shrine of strength. Find, purchase, or make symbols to affirm your triumphs and spirit strength. To impress those special qualities upon your mind, place the symbols where you'll notice them often. Change the display frequently. If each symbol is a phrase or a sentence, what story do the symbols reflect when they're positioned in a special way?

Symbols of success. What personal qualities have you developed to help you cope creatively with the challenges you have faced in the past? What do the fears you experienced earlier feel like, now that you have moved past them? What do they look like? Were they blessings in disguise? Is there an object that relates to past problems? Did special friends help you through them? What can symbolize the way you've used your skills and beliefs to transform the "demons" (fearful or unpleasant events) instead of allowing them to devour you? How have they helped you to transform parts of your personal story to empower yourself to face the next trial?

Pay attention to your life. You're stronger than you realize when you begin to examine your past from this perspective. Add these symbols of triumph to your shrine of strength or your personal medicine bag. This is the power you draw upon when something creates fear in your mind. Don't let the reaction of panic and fear rob you of your power. Don't lose your head! Look at what you've got in your medicine bag, or on your shrine.

Symbols of personal power, strength, and talent. What objects symbolize events, places, or people that in some special way affirm who you are, your power, your creativity, and the way you belong to your community and the greater environment? How would you symbolize different aspects of your personal talents, gifts, abilities? What is your gift to the world? How do you serve others? These symbols affirm yourself and connect you to your world. They belong on your shrine of strength.

How would you symbolize yourself? What objects could you use to represent different aspects of your personality? These symbols relate to you, not to the roles you play in life (spouse, sibling, friend). What makes you unique? Are you curious, a hopeless romantic, an adventurer, a warrior? Ask friends how they perceive you. You may be surprised when you contrast others' impressions with your sense of yourself.

Life line—symbols along the path of your life. Think of the major transitions within your life, extending as far back as you care to recall. Consider the significant events and the people in your life. What skills, wisdom, or other value did you gain that have contributed to the person you are today? Each value has helped in some special way with your transformation and evolution. Reflect upon these people and events and the way they've contributed to your growth.

Symbolize these "teachers" into tangible objects and attach them to a cord: you've created a "life line!" Symbolizing your history of wisdom, strength, and creativity is another way to affirm your power, your ability to survive and thrive. These seeds from the past support your continual blossoming and becoming.

Re-spirited symbols. Examine your home for signs of environmental pollution, evidenced by symbols that reflect pain from the past. If a symbol's original story is hazardous to your happiness, save the object and dump the story. Transform the significance of the object with a story to affirm some aspect of yourself or the general beauty in life. Don't let the symbol own you!

NOTES

1. Elizabeth Cogburn in a recorded presentation, "New Song May Long Dance," on a WBAI radio program, "In the Spirit," introduced by Lex Hixon, New York, May 9, 1985.

2. *David Feinstein and Stanley Krippner, Personal Mythology* (Los Angeles: Jeremy P. Tarcher, 1988), p. 178, discuss ways to create "behavioral contracts," defining them as "statements of intent to perform specific, measurable actions that are steps toward reaching a goal." This book has many excellent suggestions to determine new beliefs and ways to make changes in behavior that support them.

3. Shakti Gawain, *Creative Visualization* (New York: Bantam New Age Books, 1982), p. 10.

For Further Reading

If you're interested in reading more about David Paladin, consult the following sources.

Banerjee, H.N. *The Once and Future Life.* New York: Dell Books, 1979.

Montgomery, Ruth. *Threshold to Tomorrow.* New York: G.P. Putnam's Sons, 1982.

———. *Aliens Among Us.* New York: G.P. Putnam's Sons, 1985.

Paladin, Lynda, ed. *David "Chethlahe" Paladin, a Biography in His Words.* Box 11942, Albuquerque, New Mexico 87192-0942, 1987.

———. *Mosaic of Immortality, Insights About Death and Life.* Box 11942, Albuquerque, New Mexico 87192-0942, 1986.

Sutphen, Richard. *You Were Born Again to be Together.* New York: Pocket Books, 1976.

———. *Past Lives, Future Loves.* New York: Pocket Books, 1978.

Weisman, Alan. *We, Immortals.* Scottsdale, Arizona: Valley of the Sun Publishing Co., 1977.

For help in determining a change in attitude about some aspect of your life, you may want to read the following:

Margo Adair. *Working Inside Out.* Berkeley: Wingbow Press, 1984.

David Feinstein and Stanley Krippner. *Personal Mythology.* Los Angeles: Jeremy P. Tarcher, 1988.

Piero Ferrucci. *What We May Be.* Los Angeles: J.P. Tarcher Inc., 1982.

Eugene T. Gendlin, Ph.D. *Focusing.* New York: Bantam New Age Book, 1982.

Louise Hay. *You Can Heal Your Life.* Santa Monica, California: Hay House, 1987.

Robert A. Johnson. *Inner Work.* San Francisco: Harper & Row, Publishers, Inc., 1986.

Carol Pearson. *The Hero Within.* San Francisco: Harper and Row, Publishers, Inc., 1986.

Marsha Sinetar. *Elegant Choices, Healing Choices.* New Jersey, Paulist Press, 1988.

Bibliography

Campbell, Joseph. *The Hero With a Thousand Faces*. Cleveland: Meridian Books, The World Publishing Company, 1967.

Campbell, Joseph, with Bill Moyers. *The Power of Myth*. New York: Doubleday, 1988.

Cavendish, Richard, ed. *Man, Myth & Magic, An Illustrated Encyclopedia of the Supernatural*. New York: Marshall Cavendish Corporation, 1970.

Cirlot, J.E. *A Dictionary of Symbols*. New York: Philosophical Library, 1981.

Cogburn, Elizabeth. *New Song May Long Dance*. Recorded program, New York: WBAI radio, 1985.

Gawain, Shakti. *Creative Visualization*. New York: Bantam New Age Books, 1982.

Keen, Sam, and Anne Valley-Fox. *Your Mythic Journey*. Los Angeles: Jeremy P. Tarcher, 1989.

Sowers, Errol. Personal communication to the author, November 4, 1990.

Walker, Barbara G. *The Woman's Dictionary of Symbols and Sacred Objects*. San Francisco: Harper & Row, Publishers, 1988.

Bibliography

————. *The Woman's Encyclopedia of Myths and Secrets.* New York: Harper and Row, Publishers, Inc. 1983.

Young, Meredith Lady. *Language of the Soul: Applying Universal Principles for Self-Empowerment* (Walpole, N.H.: Stillpoint, 1987).

If you wish to contact the author, you may write to her at this address: Ceremonies, P.O. Box 11942, Albuquerque, NM 87192-0942. Please remember to enclose a stamped, self-addressed envelope if you are requesting a reply from her.

Publisher's Note

This logo represents Stillpoint's commitment to publishing books and other products that promote an enlightened value system. We seek to change human values to encourage people to live and act in accordance with a greater and more meaningful spiritual purpose and a true intent for the sanctity of all life.

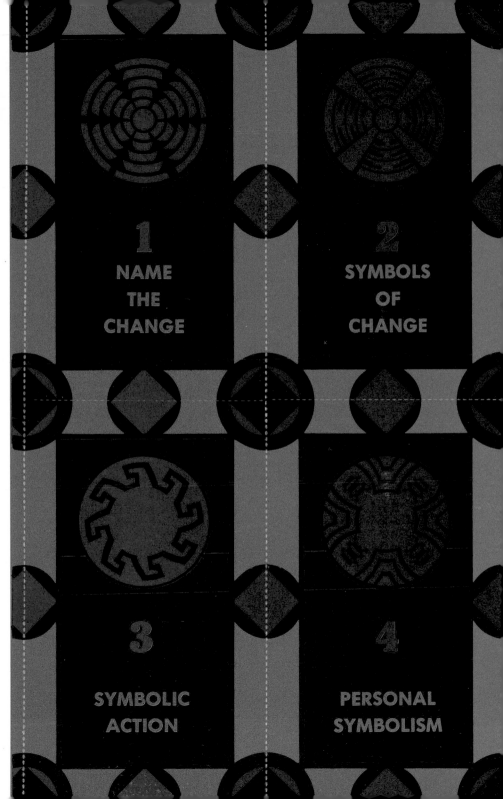

1
NAME
THE
CHANGE

2
SYMBOLS
OF
CHANGE

3
SYMBOLIC
ACTION

4
PERSONAL
SYMBOLISM

2

Symbolize What You Wish to Change

- What physical symbols or objects can you find, create, or buy that will powerfully represent what you want to change?

1

Identify the Desired Change

- What do you want to release, affirm, or celebrate?
- Can you describe the change as a wisdom story, a miracle story, or a hero story?

4

Empower Yourself with Personal Symbols

- What objects or symbols can you find, create, or buy to make your change happen, to reinforce your attitudes and commitment?
- What could represent the new person you are becoming?

3

Make the Desired Change Come Alive

- What will you do with the objects or symbols to make the desired change real for you?
- How will you act upon your symbols in order to reinforce the desired change?

5

PLACE
&
TIME

6

WITNESS

INSTRUCTIONS

BLESSING

6

Reinforce Your Ceremony with a Witness

■ Who will personally witness and/or participate in your ceremony or who will you tell about it?

5

Create the Right Time and Place

■ What kind of special environment do you wish to create for your ceremony?

■ What time would hold a particular significance for you?

**Love is the Source,
Joy is the Power,
Life is the Celebration!**

A Ceremony or Ritual is a Powerful Tool for Creating Positive Change and Healing

■ Use these ritual cards to guide your transformation from inner intention to outer results.

■ Place cards in two horizontal rows. Cards 1-6 (Planning Cards) make up the first row, cards 7-14 (Celebration Cards), the second row.

■ Begin with the Planning Cards (1-6), turning over one card at a time.

■ Use your intuition to guide you in planning each step of your ceremony. Follow the same process with the Celebration Cards (7-14).

Reinforce your own deepest intentions with the power of ceremony.

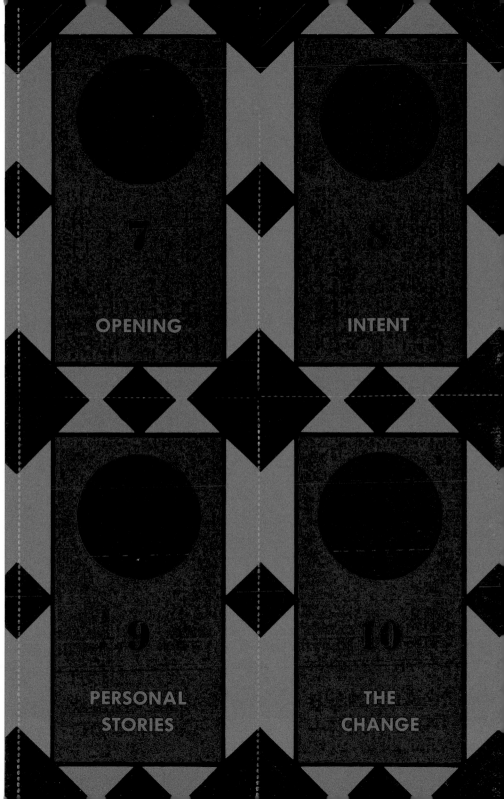

7

OPENING

8

INTENT

9

PERSONAL
STORIES

10

THE
CHANGE

8

State or Symbolize Your Intention

■ Say what you wish to change in your life.

■ Symbolize what you desire to release and/or affirm with this ceremony.

7

Choose Your Sacred Opening

■ Begin your ceremony in a sacred and meaningful way.

10

Act Out the Desired Change

■ Speak of your change and perform your symbolic act(s) of release, passage, or affirmation.

9

Infuse the Ceremony with Power

■ Talk about the significance of the symbols you selected.

■ Read meaningful passages or poems, play music, dance, sing songs, or tell stories to launch your ceremony.

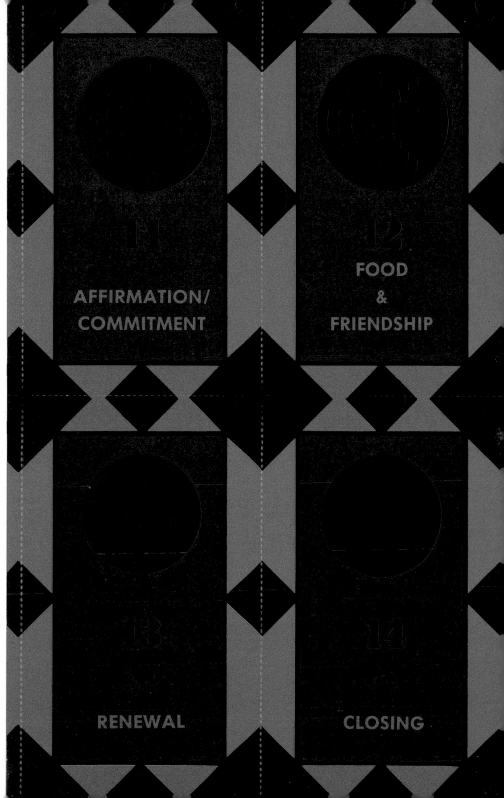

11

AFFIRMATION/
COMMITMENT

12

FOOD
&
FRIENDSHIP

13

RENEWAL

14

CLOSING

12

Share and Express Gratitude

■ Celebrate the beginning of your new change with food and/or drink, gift-giving, toasting, or more readings, songs, or music.

11

Make Your Commitment Live

■ Through a significant act make your commitment to the new way of being and/or thinking.

14

Give Thanks and Honor the Energies of Creation

■ Thank those who shared in your ceremony, honor the ceremony process. Take symbolic action(s) to bring the ceremony to a close.

13

Reaffirm the New Change

■ Affirm and symbolize your new beginning.

■ Reinforce the process of positive change.